Enjoy Nigeria

(A Travel Guide)

Ian Nason

Spectrum Books Limited
Ibadan. Owerri. Kaduna

Published by
Spectrum Books Limited
Sunshine House
Second Commercial Road
Oluyole Estate
Ibadan, Nigeria

in association with
Safari Books (Export) Limited
Bell Royal House
Hilgrove Street
St Helier, Jersey
Channel Island, UK

© Ian Nason 1991

All rights reserved. This book is copyright and
so no part of it may be reproduced, stored in a
retrieval system or transmitted in any form or by
any means, electronic, mechanical, electrostatic,
magnetic tape, photocopying, recording, or otherwise
without the express permission of the author
who is the copyright owner.

First published 1991

ISBN 978 - 246 - 108 - 3

Printed by Intec Printers Limited, Ibadan

Dedication

I dedicate this book to the people of Bakana Island, Rivers State, who conferred on me the Honorary Chieftaincy title of Aku Tubo of Bakana in March 1990. Also to the Nigerian Conservation Foundation whose efforts to protect the flora and fauna of Nigeria for its future generations deserve every encouragement.

Contents

	Acknowledgements	vii
	Foreword	ix
	Introduction	xi
1.	**Lagos**	1
2.	**South-West**	8
	The area south-west of the River Niger	
3.	**South-East**	43
	The area south-east of the Niger and Benue Rivers	
4.	**North-West**	68
	The area north of the River Niger which includes the states of Niger, Sokoto, Kaduna, Kano, Katsina and the Federal Capital Territory	
5.	**North-East**	95
	The area north of the River Benue including the states of Borno, Bauchi, Plateau and parts of Benue and Gongola	
6.	**Across-Border Travel**	116
	Benin, Cameroon, Togo, Mali and Niger	
7.	**Countries On A direct Flight From Nigeria**	135
	Egypt, Kenya, Zimbabwe, Brazil and England	

Intec Printers Limited

(THE QUALITY COLOUR PRINTERS)

Producer of:

* COLOUR CALENDARS
* COLOUR SEPARATIONS
* BROCHURES
* BOOKS
* MAGAZINES
* DIARIES

Quality Printing First

KILOMETRE 8
OLD LAGOS ROAD
P M B 5332 IBADAN NIGERIA
☎ 313377 · 311678

Acknowledgements

Firstly, I must thank my dear wife, who has been my companion on many of my travels, for patiently typing, correcting, proof reading and bearing with me over this whole project, which has been far more demanding than I had ever imagined. I must also thank those who have sent me reports of tourist sites and directed me to them. Amongst these are Tasso Leventis of the Leventis Group; Les Hodgson, the former Manager of African Timber and Plywood at Sapele, Paul Williams and George Edgar, both of the British High Commission, Lagos, who are intrepid travellers and have charted new routes for others to follow.

I have received advice, encouragement and sound criticism from many others which have forced me to re-check my information and redouble my efforts towards finding suitable tourist sites, not only for the international community, but also for the domestic market, as without a sound domestic market demanding high standards, tourism will fail to realise its full potential in Nigeria. For this advice, I owe a debt to Colonel Tony Ukpo, Principal Staff Officer to the President; Hajia Zainab Duke, an author who suggested the more positive title of *Enjoy Nigeria,* and Tom Harris of the British High Commission who has my doubtful gratitude for suggesting that I write a travel brief in the first place!

Further thanks must go to all those who helped to sell my original three travel booklets called *Travel Nigeria.* Without their help I would never have attempted this book. Although I am unable to mention the names of everybody who contributed in the preparation of this book, I would particularly like to pay tribute to Fons and Leny Claessen, the joint Secretaries of the Nigerian Field Society (NFS); Ros Pearce, of NFS; Sandra Forsyth of the British Wives Group; John Pease of Schlumberger, Port Harcourt; Lt Colonel Albert Beraud from France and Brigadier Habib from Egypt and other fellow Defence Advisers who checked the manuscript, and Freddie Scott of the West Africa Committee, who was responsible for putting me in touch with Spectrum Books and many of the advertisers.

Finally, I must thank my sponsors who have kindly advertised in this book. Without their help the book could not have 'taken off'. I hope the success of the book will reward them for their backing.

No book can reach the market place without a good publisher. Joop Berkhout and Spectrum Books receive my admiration for running the usual commercial risks by accepting *Enjoy Nigeria*

I apologise if I have left anyone out, but to everyone else who has helped I send my grateful thanks.

State House
Lagos
Nigeria

15th June, 1990

Chief Colonel I.G. Nason, OSC (Nig) N.D.C., p.sc
Defence Adviser
British High Commission
LAGOS

Dear Ian,

1. I was delighted to have my attention drawn to your work titled: "Enjoy Nigeria".

2. At a time when we are hoping to promote our tourist industry in order to boost foreign exchange earnings, at a time when Nigerians and the world at large are becoming increasingly aware of the scenic beauty and the cultural riches of this nation, I consider your work both timely and apt.

3. It is my hope, however, that in view of the dynamic nature of progress, this fascinating piece of work will be periodically up-dated, to encapsulate new developments.

4. I commend your efforts and wish you every success.

Yours Sincerely

Signed
General Ibrahim B Babangida
President
Commander-In-Chief
Armed Forces of Nigeria

Introduction

General

In 1979, when I first came to Nigeria, I found that many people had a wealth of travel information in their heads but had put little down on paper. I therefore produced 'A Newcomer's Guide to Kaduna' with a request at the end asking readers to write up their travel experiences and include the notes in the back of the guide. This my contemporaries in Kaduna did most enthusiastically, and on returning to Nigeria in 1987, I was delighted to see that the idea had been expanded and a booklet called, 'The British Advisory Team Travel Notes' was in circulation. It is now time to expand again and also to update some of the information, which is constantly changing as Nigeria develops new roads, hotels and tourist assets.

My thanks must go to the many people who have written up their own trips in order that others can avoid some of the pitfalls of travel in Nigeria and neighbouring countries. The pioneer traveller in Nigeria has a difficult time even after taking advice. Only major roads are signed, (although this situation is improving), maps are often inaccurate, the wet season rains or dry season harmattan can blemish a journey and the numerous police, customs, immigration and local government road blocks all add to the difficulties and delays encountered. Add to those the occasional enormous car-damaging potholes and eroded road sides, the risk of accident and the unpredictable taxi driver ('Let Them Say!'), who would dare to venture outside the relative security of his own home? The fact that we do is because there is so much to see and do in Nigeria. It is my intention to show you how much you are missing if you do not travel in and around Nigeria. It is a fascinating country with a vast range of landscapes from the mangrove swamps of the delta area to the semi-arid Sahel region of the north, with a corresponding change in the lifestyles of the people.

Scope

To keep these notes simple there is little information on the geography, history, climate or culture of Nigeria, but there are many books covering these matters, e.g.: *Nigeria, Giant of Africa,* by Peter Holmes; *The Living Arts of Nigeria,* by William Fagg; *Nigeria,* by Jaqueline Redith; *Nigeria, The Land, Its Art and its People - an Anthology* by Frederick Lumley; and *Nigeria, the Land and its People* by Richard Synge. These books can fill some of the gaps in our knowledge, and if they are not available in bookshops, they may be found in libraries such as the British Council Library in Kingsway Road, Lagos.

I have divided Nigeria into 4 regions rather than covering each state separately, to make it easier for the traveller. The regions will be further divided into areas around main towns as these towns usually have the best hotels. The towns are listed in alphabetical order. Most of the journeys will be based on travel from Lagos. In the case of journeys outside Nigeria, I have confined myself to the most popular journeys to neighbouring countries, and those to which you can fly direc from Lagos.

A simple guidebook like this cannot possibly cover all the tourist spots, roads, accommodation and distances. I apologise in advance for any mistakes in detail, routes, etc., because it would be impossible to keep it completely up-to-date. Nevertheless, the information is the best available at the time of writing. I have not included many maps, because they may not include all the details, (and that is beyond the scope of this guide); maps can be confusing. I have found during my years in Nigeria that, with few exceptions, if you ask the local people you will get the right answer and they often go out of their way to help, even to the extent of offering to guide you themselves.

Information

There are a number of vital pieces of information that everyone wants to know when travelling, so the following will be included: roads, routes, timings, accommodation, the tourist site itself, and miscellaneous information. Costs are not included because they change so often and can confuse the tourist. Take up-to-date advice.

Preparation

It is worth carrying out some form of preparation before travelling. Time must be made to check on spare tyres, tyre pump, jack, spares like fan belts, etc., petrol cans for some more remote parts of Nigeria, or when there is a temporary distribution problem; or for neighbouring countries, documents, maps, compass, torch, tools, tow rope, first aid pack, insect repellant, an emergency food supply and drinks. Remember that water is vital in the tropics. You may feel comfortable in your air-conditioned car when all is well, but what happens if it breaks down and you are kilometres away from any village, wrestling with a puncture in the mid-day sun? Always plan on the worst case, especially with children. When you are travelling with children remember to take some car games and books. However, do not overload your car; you will probably regret it when your car meets a large pothole! It is advisable to take emergency telephone numbers with you, and leave a copy of your route with a friend.

Documentation

Inside Nigeria

It is wise to carry the following documents:
   a. Valid driving licence (Nigerian).
   b. Driving licence from your country of origin, for expatriates.
   c. Passport or identity card for hotels.
   d. Third party insurance.
   e. Car registration document.

Outside Nigeria

Crossing borders can be slow, because of the documentation and registration of all your personal details and car details in a book at Customs and Excise and Immigration points on both sides of the border. Any journey times must allow at least one hour for each border crossing although it can be done in less time. Apart from the documents for Nigeria you need the following:

a. International Certificate for Motor Vehicles from the Lagos Police Headquarters, Moloney Street, Lagos.
b. International Driving Licence (1920 and 1949) from your country of origin or Police Headquarters in Lagos. (Not always necessary but you could be caught without it).
c. Brown Card for third party insurance in West Africa. This is not valid for Cameroon, which is in Central Africa. You should obtain third party insurance once you are in Cameroon.
d. Visas: check if these are required through the Embassy of the country you wish to visit. Remember to check, if you are an expatriate in Nigeria, that your Nigerian visa is valid for re-entry. British passport holders do not need a visa for Niger.
e. A letter of free passage is useful if you know someone important who is a national of the country you are visiting.
f. Currency of the country you are visiting, e.g. West African CFAs for Francophone countries, but Central African CFA's for Cameroon. Some small coins or notes for tolls, tips, etc. are always useful. Traveller's cheques are accepted in the best hotels, but credit cards are only accepted in a few.
g. Vaccination certificates for yellow fever. Always check with the embassy of the country you are visiting, as regulations can change if there is a cholera outbreak, for example.
h. If you are a visitor and have not got a Residence Permit, you are likely to be asked to pay for hotels in Nigeria in hard currency. All hotels require a substantial deposit on arrival.

Fuel, Water and Medicine

Fuel is usually readily available in Nigeria, except in the more remote areas, but occasionally there are local shortages particularly at Christmas time, or when a refinery is temporarily out of action. So it is sometimes necessary to take jerrycans. In Cameroon, Benin, Togo, Niger and Mali, fuel is less readily available; it is also more expensive. It is always worth taking some fuel in jerrycans to these countries. In Ghana fuel is sometimes difficult to find, so fill up in Togo to keep you going until you can obtain some. It would be advisable to check with the Ghanaian High Commission in Lagos about the situation.

Water is essential if you are camping. If you are staying in hotels it is still useful to have some bottled water, or you can order it from the hotel, as the water in plastic bottles in hotel fridges is usually tap water. Never be without water on a journey in case of a puncture or breakdown when you might have to exert yourself in the heat. Lack of water and salt can lead to dehydration, with resulting headaches, cramp and in a bad case, heat exhaustion, which needs medical attention. Salt is vital in the tropics when you are sweating a great deal.

A first-aid kit is essential for cuts, stings, stomach illnesses, headaches and sunburn. A lotion for dry skin is useful in the north during the dry season when skin can become as parched as the landscape. With the risk of AIDS, it is worth taking a kit for blood transfusions in case of accident. Take your own anti-malarial prophylactics and any drugs and pills you might need as medicines are not always available locally.

Up-to-date Information

It is commonsense, but it is worth mentioning - do ask around your friends and contacts before setting out on a major expedition to say, Timbuktu, Agadez or Cameroon, just to check on the essentials. Roads may have either improved or deteriorated, a border crossing may have been closed or a new document required. It would be frustrating indeed to drive 1,000 km to find that you are missing some vital document or the map is wrong and there is no border crossing after all - we found this in Cameroon. Luckily, there was an alternative route, though a somewhat hazardous one. Usually when you are faced with such a problem, there is a way around it, but sometimes it is expensive, time-consuming and extremely tedious when you want to get on your way.

The People

In our experience, the people in Nigeria are incredibly friendly and cheerful. They love a laugh and have a great sense of fun. They are always willing to help, sometimes at great inconvenience to themselves so do not be afraid to ask. Remember that in a hot climate tempers can fray very quickly, but a joke can often dissipate a potentially difficult situation. Nigerians love giving and receiving gifts, so be prepared by taking gifts with you, particularly something from your own country.

If you have received assistance you will be expected to pay some 'dash', but if a large service is involved, e.g. pushing your car out of the mud, negotiate with the village headman or the people concerned beforehand to prevent arguments later. Do not be pushy when you go into a village or sacred area. Always take the advice of the village headman or spokesman. There are certain things you are not allowed to see or photograph. Do not insist or sneak a photograph, as this could cause serious offence. Be careful about photography. In general, ask before photograhing people, especially women. Do not photograph government buildings, military installations or border areas. Binoculars can be mistaken for a camera, so bird-watchers, beware! Finally, when seeking information, always exchange greetings before asking directly for assistance, as this is the Nigerian custom.

Summary

In order to enjoy a trouble-free journey in Nigeria or neighbouring countries it is essential to plan and prepare. You will never regret finding the time to prepare your car and collect the essentials: food, water, maps, documents and especially medical requirements. For those who are used to travelling in Europe and America, there are a number of differences to travelling in West Africa. You are travelling in an area where not all the roads are signed, where communication is sparse, accommodation is not always up to the standard of the international traveller, and where documentation at border crossings can be slow and tedious. If you do get into difficulties, there are few breakdown trucks, few road patrolmen, no ambulances on alert and few well-equipped garages. I emphasise that this is not a criticism of Nigeria or West Africa, but 'Rome was not built in a day'. West Africa is still developing and full facilities are not yet available for the tourist.

The answer is:
   a. Drive carefully and defensively, beware of the unpredictable and it is advisable **not to drive at night**.
   b. Take all you need for yourself and passengers, especially children.
   c. Take all you need for your car.
   d. Have great patience and a sense of humour.

Safe Journey!

1
Lagos

General

Lagos is the present capital of Nigeria, until the seat of government moves to the Federal Capital Territory at Abuja. Lagos has a life of its own and is completely different from other cities in Nigeria. At present, it houses the President and his departments of State. It is the headquarters for many parastatals and national institutions. There is also a large commercial community, and a colourful Diplomatic Corps which adds a cosmopolitan flavour to the city.

The city is a mass of human activity, day and night. Moving around is sometimes a slow and painful process, whether on foot or by car, owing to the hustle and bustle of so many people, all seemingly in an enormous hurry. Few vehicles do not carry signs of the bruising battles fought at every road junction, roundabout and bottleneck. It is a frenetic existence until the Lagosian gains the sanctuary of his own home. Some control over the traffic is gained by limiting the cars on the road on Mondays, Wednesdays and Fridays to those with numberplates beginning with odd numbers, and those on Tuesdays and Thursdays with numberplates beginning with even numbers.

Lagos still has many fine old colonial buildings both in the government and residential parts of the city, but many are now being replaced by large office blocks and flats, the necessary scourge of all modern cities with limited space for expansion. Fortunately, the city has many waterways running through it which provide much needed open spaces amidst the concrete jungle. One or two fine buildings stand out, e.g. the National Theatre, the Anglican Church of Nigeria Cathedral, the Central Mosque and the Law Courts.

There is little you cannot buy in Lagos, but you have to know where to look. There are department stores in central Lagos and Apapa, smaller supermarkets and specialist shops in the residential suburbs and a fascinating variety of markets. Tinubu Square and Balogun markets are in central Lagos. Tinubu Square is the main cloth market, including imported furnishing materials. Balogun market in Martins Street has clothing, shoes, jewellery, cassettes, etc. Jankara Market, in Okoya Street, has an interesting 'juju stall', where ingredients for traditional medicines are sold. Yaba has a large two-storeyed market building where you can also buy furnishing materials. Alaba Market along the Badagry Road sells a multitude of goods, including electrical and household goods, camera equipment and furniture. It is advisable not to be too ostentatious with money or jewellery when visiting these markets. For local handicrafts like carvings, baskets, beads, malachite, leatherware and cloth, there are traders' stalls outside the large hotels, but as usual, hard bargaining is essential. Recently, the old Bar Beach Market has been moved to a site along the Lekki road amongst the new housing estate at the Lekki Beach roundabout. It sells tourist items, as well as fruits, vegetables, groceries and drinks. Apapa is a good shopping area as the large stores and the market are all nearby.

Near Lagos there are several sandy beaches along the Atlantic Coast which stretch for hundreds of kilometres to the east and west. However, there is a very strong undertow and great care must be taken as even strong swimmers have drowned on these beaches; so treat the sea with the greatest respect.

The wet season is longer in Lagos than in the north of Nigeria, and lasts from April to October with occasional storms outside this period. The hottest time is February to March, when the harmattan has usually receded and the rains have not begun.

Lagos is well-served by international and national airlines and has an expressway north to Ibadan and access to the Benin Expressway through either Shagamu or Epe. It is only a 2-hour drive to the border with the Benin Republic.

Tourist sites

For a capital city, Lagos is not as well-endowed with tourist sites as some other cities in Nigeria. Nevertheless, the sites that should interest a tourist are:

1. Art and Crafts

a. The *National Museum,* Onikan, near Tafawa Balewa Square. This museum is of great interest to any one interested in African art who wishes to understand the rich cultural heritage of Nigeria. Artefacts in the museum date back to 500BC - 200AD in the case of the beautiful Nok terracotta heads. The museum is well-laid out to show the development of the various cultures throughout the centuries of Nigeria's history. Sometimes, the museum has exhibitions of art, and there is a craft village and museum kitchen at the back of the compound. It is open from 9.00am to 6.00pm every day and prepares Nigerian dishes.

b. *National Gallery of Modern Art,* National Theartre, Iganmu.Go in through entrance 'C'. Artwork from Nigeria's leading artist is on display. It is of interest to those who have not seen African art before as it is fascinating to see how the art forms differ from those in Europe and America. It is open from 9.00 am until 5.00 pm, Monday to Friday. At weekends you must apply to the management in writing one week in advance for it to be opened, but I suspect that it would be easier to go during the week.

c. *National Gallery of Crafts and Design,* Opposite Gate 'C' of the National Theatre and is open from 9.00 a.m until 5.00 p.m except on weekends.

d. The *Didi Museum* in Akin Adesola Street, is open from Monday to Saturday, 10.00 am until 5.00 pm. This small, privately-owned art collection, attractively displayed in a modern gallery, houses works of art by contemporary Nigerian artists as well as some African antiques, including bronzes, terracotta figures and wood carvings. The exhibits are changed frequently, to add variety.

2. Beaches

a. The main beach on Victoria Island is *Victoria Beach,* (usually known as Bar Beach) alongside Ahmadu Bello Road. It is very dangerous for swimming and it is not recommended. On public holidays it is crowded with Nigerians, who make a day of it. So it is a colourful scene, as people dress up for the occasion. It is not advisable to take valuables onto the beach. At present the beach is being gradually washed away be the sea.

b. *Tarkwa Bay.* A sheltered beach within the harbour breakwater. You get there by a 'Tarzan' boat from Maroko or 'Fiki' boat from under Falomo Bridge on Victoria Island. The beach is a pleasant outing and has safe bathing even for small children. You can hire deck chairs and an awning on the beach, and there are traders selling pineapples, coconuts and many other items. Take your own food, cold drinks and suncream. There are plenty of young boys to carry your possessions. *Lighthouse beach* is beyond Tarkwa. It is a lovely open beach, but can be dangerous for swimming. Do not take jewellery, watches or cameras on the beach, especially if you walk away from the crowded areas.

c. Beaches along the Lekki peninsula. The first, *Lekki Beach,* is only a few kilometres from the city. Take the road past the 1004 flats along the Maroko Road to the Lekki Peninsula, and at the third roundabout it is signposted to the right, along a new road. The charge is ₦5 for a car and ₦1 per person. It is possible to hire a beach shelter made of palmfronds. The bathing is dangerous, so great care must be taken.

Maiyegun Beach is signed on the right just after the third roundabout. Access is along a sandy track which may not be suitable for all types of vehicles.

Eleko Beach was opened in 1989, and is further along the Lekki Peninsula, approximately 50 km from Lagos, just past the 'Epe 22' km post. It is signed to the right along a new-sealed road which extends for 4 km to the beach. At the time of writing, this beach is quieter and there are fewer traders, but this situation may not last. There are other beaches, but these are only available by 4-wheel drive vehicles at present.

d. *Badagry Beach* is one hour's drive along the Badagry Road towards Cotonou in the Benin Republic. It is possible to go by boat to both Badagry and *Agaja* beaches, but the journey is expensive, unless you have your own boat.

Hotels

The recommended hotels are:

a. *Sheraton Hotel,* Airport Road, Ikeja, Tel: 900931 (the Lagos code is 01). Said to be the best in Lagos, but it is some distance from the centre and the main residential area. Driving between the Sheraton and the main centres of commerce on Lagos Island can be slow and difficult, but the hotel is very convenient for the airport and the industrial areas of Ikeja. It has a swimming pool.

b. *L'Hotel Eko Meridien* (previously called Eko Holiday Inn), Karamo Waters, Victoria Island. Tel: 615000. The most popular with overseas visitors, and recommended if you are visiting central Lagos. Has an excellent Chinese Restaurant on the top floor. There is a pleasant swimming pool.

c. The *Federal Palace Hotel*, Ahmadu Bello Way, Victoria Island. Tel: 610031. Has a good Italian restaurant in the basement, and a very good Chinese restaurant in the main hotel.

d. The *Ikoyi Hotel*, Kingsway Road, Ikoyi. Tel: 603200. Also has a good Chinese Restaurant, which is not smart, but the food is very good.

None of these hotels are expensive for those paid in hard currencies, but not cheap if you are on the local economy. Most of the hotels have traders' stalls outside, where you can buy local handicrafts, but you need to bargain hard. Visitors without residence permits will have to pay their hotel bills in hard currency. There are restaurants to suit all tastes in Lagos. It is impossible to mention them all, but this is a selection.

a. *The Brasserie*, 52 Adetokunbo Ademola Street. Tel: 615464. There is continental cuisine on the ground floor and an Indian restaurant on the first floor.

b. *The Bagatelle:* 208/212 Broad Street (fourth floor), Lagos Island, Tel: 662410. Excellent service.

Mothers...

Here's a new one from Glaxo

babeena
Baby Milk Cereal

It's a proud moment when you have a baby.
First, you'll start him on mother's milk – nature's best food for baby; but from 4 months baby needs to be introduced to solid foods. That's when to choose Glaxo's new Babeena Baby Milk Cereal. Babeena Baby Milk Cereal, in banana flavour, is just the food for your baby.

Babeena Baby Milk Cereal is full of tasty goodness, your baby will love every spoonful. Made from maize, rice, soyabeans and milk, it contains a high level of protein, a proper amino acid balance and recommended levels of minerals and vitamins. So Babeena will provide a highly balanced easily digested meal that has everything your baby needs to grow strong, fit and healthy.

Babeena's so easy to prepare too ...add clean water that's been boiled and cooled, stir... and it's ready to eat! Fresh, smooth, tasty and nourishing.

Mother ...show your baby you care by giving him Babeena Baby Milk Cereal.
Your baby'll love you for it.

Price: ₦18.50

babeena...*Baby's nourishing start in solids.*

c. *Jaws Seaford Restaurant,* Plot 8 Ozumba Mbadiwe Road, Vic-Island. Mostly Chinese food.

d. *The Lagoon,* 1c Ozumba Mbadiwe, Victoria Island, Tel: 611616. Naturally, it overlooks the Lagoon, and the food is good.

e. *The Sherlaton,* 108 Awolowo Road, which serves Indian food. Tel: 681911.

f. *The Koreana,* 81 Awolowo Road which serves Korean, Japanese and Chinese food. Tel: 681402.

g. *The Water Gardens,* 55 Awolowo Road, Chinese and Lebanese food. Tel: 681333.

Recommended books

The following books are recommended for more and detailed information about Lagos and its environ:

a. *Survive Lagos* by Elizabeth Cox and Erica Anderssen.

b. *Nigeria Tourist Guide,* obtainable from the Maison de France, Plot PC 14, off Idowu Taylor Street, Victoria Island. Tel: 615592.

c. *Spectrum Road Map,* 1990 edition.

2
The South-West

General

South-west Nigeria covers the area bordered by the Benin Republic in the west, the River Niger in the north and east and the Gulf of Guinea/Bight of Benin in the south. The southern part of this region consists mainly of rain forest, oil palm and rubber plantations, the snaking rivers and mangrove swamps of the delta area and the long sandy beaches of the Atlantic coast. As you travel north towards the Niger the landscape changes slowly to guinea savanna, dotted with hills and inselbergs (granite outcrops). This

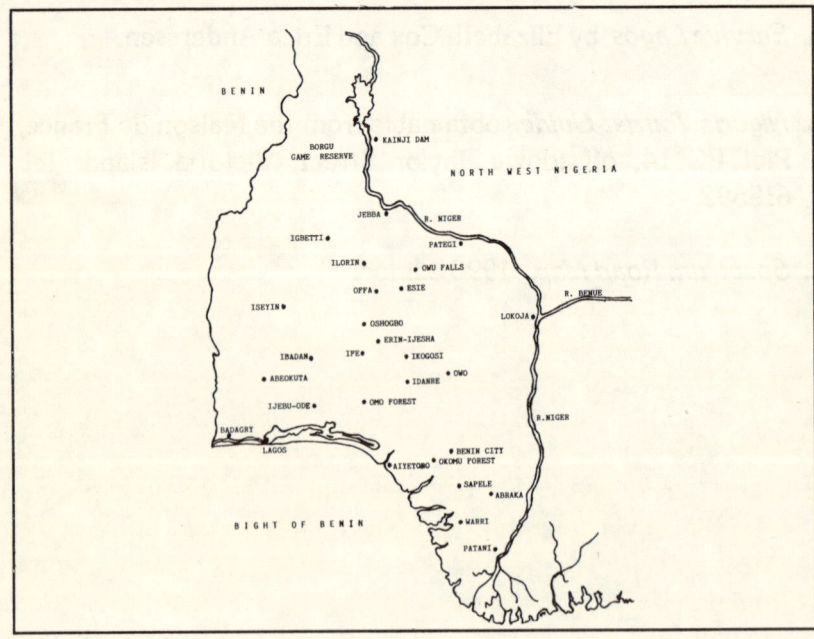

area includes some of the largest cities in Nigeria, historical towns and shrines, a game reserve, some excellent museums, fascinating markets with some superb craftwork, besides many other places of interest.

South-west Nigeria also saw the first appearance of Europeans in the area, starting with the Portuguese in the 16th century followed by the palm-oil traders and English, Scottish and German missionaries who set up their first mission post at Badagry, west of Lagos in the 19th century. Sadly this area was also infamous for the slave trade which began before the appearance of the Europeans but was fully exploited by them. The trade, fortunately, was stopped by the British, but not without great suffering. Relics of the trade at the old slave posts are still to be seen along the coast, especially at Ouidah (pronounced Weedah) in the Benin Republic.

Abeokuta

General

Abeokuta is a Yoruba town with a mixed Christian and Muslim population. It is a historical town both for the Yoruba and for the early Christian missionaries who moved there from Badagry on the coast. The name Abeokuta, meaning 'under the rock', is derived from the Olumo Rock, which is the town's most famous landmark. Abeokuta is the capital of Ogun State and has a traditional ruler, the Alake of Egbaland. The town is built on the Ogun River between a number of rocky hills, and is therefore attractive photographically. It has several interesting markets and it is here that the traditional *adire* cloth is made.

Tourist sites

a. *Olumo Rock.* This rock, considered sacred by the Egba people, is on the east side of the Ogun River, close to the centre of the town. When you reach the white-painted stone obelisk 'roundabout' near the market, turn right at the sign (north) and the entrance to the rock is on the right a few hundred metres along this road. Everyone in Abeokuta knows where the rock is, so you can ask for direction. It is suggested that you take a guide from the tourist centre at the bottom of the rock, if they are available, who will show you the old living quarters in the caves used in the Yoruba civil wars as a sanctuary, and also conduct you to the top, where you can get an excellent view of Abeokuta and the Ogun river. There are steps to the caves and the shrine (where festivals are held and sacrifices offered), but after that the climb is fairly steep and it is essential to wear sensible shoes like trainers or desert boots. Take your camera as the scene from the summit is very impresive. In 1990, construction was in progress to provide more facilities for tourists at the base of the rock.

b. *The Market.* The local populace, the Egba, are keen traders. The market sells the traditional *adire* cloth which is made by a process similar to batik, but cassava starch is used instead of wax for applying the patterns and the material is then dyed in indigo, creating the beautiful blue and indigo cloth. Batick materials are also made at this market, using a variety of coloured dyes. The main cloth market is in the centre of the town; near the white stone obelisk.

c. *Ijaye Pottery.* The pottery stall is on the side of the road in the centre of the town, and has a large variety of interesting pots for sale. Ask in the market for directions.

d. *The Oba's Palace.* The official residence of the Alake of Egbaland is in Ake, a district of Abeokuta. On request you may be allowed to see around the palace, including the Throne Room which has a Bible presented by King Edward VII, and another by the present Queen of England. Wole Soyinka, the celebrated author who won the Nobel Prize for Literature (1986), was brought up in Ake where his father was a headmaster, and has given the name, Ake, to the first volume of his autobiography. It is a beautifully descriptive book.

Hotels

The *Ogun State Hotel* is the main hotel in Abeokuta and has a pleasant view of the town. There is a swimming pool and poolside bar for refreshments. A visit to Abeokuta can make a good day's outing from Lagos.

Route

The best route from Lagos is via the Ibadan expressway. Turn off the expressway at Shagamu (about half-way), where it is signed to Abeokuta, and continue west until you reach the town. The journey takes less than 2 hours. To vary the route back to Lagos, take the old road, the A5 through Ifo, Otta and Ikeja. Both roads are good. Fruits and vegetables can be bought on the side of the road much more cheaply than in Lagos.

Abraka

General

Abraka is a tourist resort with a Motel, on the Ethiope River in Bendel State about 100 km from Benin City. The crystal clear river which is fed by a spring, flows through a beautiful forested area. The Abraka River Resort Motel has a sandy beach on the river with tables and umbrellas, and you can hire boats to row yourself, or if you prefer, you can hire local canoes with a boy to paddle you upstream. It is fun to go up river and float back to the Motel in a rubber ring (inner tube) which can be hired from the Motel. The water is safe for swimming, and it is so clear that you can see the fish at the bottom 5 m or so, below. There are several private beaches with beach huts along the river, belonging to large companies. A visit to Abraka is well worthwhile, especially with children, as you can have a safe swim and there is plenty to occupy both adults and children in an attractive setting.

Route

From Benin City take the Sapele Road from the central roundabout. Near Sapele you cross a large bridge. Then instead of turning right at the T-junction for Sapele, turn towards **Warri** and soon afterwards there is a left turning off the main road towards Abraka. When you reach Abraka, the Motel is to the left down a laterite road, but as it is unsigned, the best method is to ask for the Motel when you reach the town. Journey time from **Benin** is about $1\frac{1}{2}$ hours and from Lagos it is about 5 hours.

Hotels

The *Abraka River Resort Motel* is right on the river with apartments and parking space for your car. There is also parking space for day visitors. At busy holiday periods the service can be rather slow. If you have children, it may be worth bringing some of their own favourite foods. Tel: (054) 66140.

Aiyetoro Commune Village

General

Aiyetoro Village was founded as a religious commune in 1945 and was once entirely self-supporting, with everything being owned collectively. Since the death of its leader, however, the community has been less structured, and now everything is owned individually. The village which is on the Ondo coastline, is interesting for its social history, but the appearance and atmosphere of the village is changing. Aiyetoro (meaning 'world of peace') is on a strip of land between the sea and the lagoon and is connected by bridges which are necessary in the wet season. It can only be approached by boat from Igbo-Koda, and the 55 minute journey in a fast boat is a very pleasant part of the outing, as much of the journey is through swamp forest and there are picturesque villages on stilts en route. Take a picnic lunch pack and plenty of water as well as hats and suncream for those with fair skin. It is a full day's outing from Lagos, so start early in the morning. Visitors are advised to pay a courtesy call on the Oba, or one of his staff.

Route

Drive east out of Victoria Island down the Lekki Peninsula to Epe and from there to the Benin expressway at Ijebu-Ode. Turn right onto the expressway and continue until you reach Ore (about 205 km). Turn right (south) and drive to Okitipupa (about 40 km). Just before the town, turn left at a T-junction with a statue of a boy carrying a bunch of palm kernels on his head. Turn right in Okitipupa where it is signed to Igbo-Koda, and on reaching the village drive straight on until you reach the jetty where you hire a boat for the journey by water to Aiyetoro. Negotiate the price for your journey before you start. In 1990, the best price was ₦200 per boat which could seat about 6-7 people, after hard bargaining. From Ikeja, the best way to the Benin Expressway is via the Ibadan expressway and Shagamu.

Badagry

General

Badagry in Lagos State, on the coast, west of Lagos, was the first town settled by missionaries in Nigeria. The 'First Storey House' (the first two-storey building in the country) erected by the missionaries, is still standing and is due to be refurbished. The well-kept graveyard was the final resting place of missionaries from Scotland, England and Germany and you can still see their names on the gravestones. Most missionaries entered Nigeria from the east, through Calabar, but Badagry has the distinction of being the first mission post in the country. From here the missionaries moved north to Abeokuta. In the slave-trading days, many slaves were shipped from Badagry, and there are still some relics of this terrible trade in the town. Badagry, therefore, is of more interest to historians than the tourist. There are pleasant beaches nearby along the coast, but again, remember that the sea is dangerous and great care must be taken.

Route

From Lagos Island go round the National Theatre towards Festac Village and onto the Badagry expressway. It is about 1 hour's journey in the direction of the border with the Benin Republic.

Benin City

General

Benin City (pronounced Beneen or Bini) is the capital of Bendel State and is steeped in history. The world-renowned Benin bronzes date back to the 15th century when the Oba of Benin ruled the large and powerful Edo kingdom. Bronze making was an art used for the glorification of the Oba. In 1897, a British expeditionary force sacked Benin and carried away many of the finest bronzes to London. This unfortunate incident was as a result of the ambush and murder of the British representatives on their way to visit the Oba in Benin. Consequently, the Oba was banished to Calabar, but the family was reinstated later by the British. The present Oba is a direct descendant. Some of the bronzes which were removed to England are on display in the British Museum (see Chapter 7) where they are admired by people from all over the world, but there are several fine ex-examples of the bronzes in both the Benin and Lagos Museums, especially the latter. Today, bronze-making is still continued in several streets in the city.

Tourist sites

a. The *Oba's Palace* is in the centre of the city, south-west of the central roundabout and it is possible to visit it if a request is made to the Oba's secretary. Festivals are held here throughout the year, but the most important ones are towards the end of the year, in December.

b. *The Benin Museum* is situated in the middle of the large central roundabout in the city. It contains examples of the famous bronzes and other historical artefacts. It is open daily from 9.00 am to 6.00 pm including Sundays. It is proposed to open a Museum kitchen serving Nigerian food.

c. *Bronze craft.* There are several streets where bronze making by the 'lost wax' process is still practised, including Igun and Oloton Streets. Igun Street is first left off Sakpoba Road, just past Leventis Stores at the central roundabout. Samson Aigbe's workshop is on the left, in Igun Street. O Omodamwen & Sons Art Gallery and workshop is at 7, Oloton Street, off Oba Market Road.

d. *Wood carvers.* Again, there are several streets where woodcarvers are to be found, but the main one is on the Airport Road, close to the Oba's Palace.

e. *Oba's market* This is an extensive market near the Oba's Palace. All the above places of interest are in the centre of the town, near the central roundabout, so it is very convenient.

f. *Chief Ogiamen's House.* This is situated at 97 Sakpoba Road, which is off the central roundabout. As the sign outside his house says, 'This is a fine example of Benin traditional architecture built before 1897. It is unique in that no building of a comparable status survived intact the Great Fire which occured at the time and destroyed a great part of the city.' It is possible to obtain permission to visit this house through the curator of the museum, or the Chief himself if he is in residence.

g. *Benin Moat.* Originally the town was defended by a deep moat, stretching right round the city, parts of which are still visible today, and would be of interest to historians. There are plans to renovate these very significant earthworks.

Route

From Lagos, the journey takes about three and a half hours. From Victoria Island or Ikoyi the best route is along the Lekki Peninsula to Epe, then to Ijebu-Ode where you turn right onto the Benin expressway. Continue for over 200 km until you reach Benin City. From Ikeja, take the Ibadan expressway to Shagamu and turn right onto the Benin expressway.

Hotels

The *Country Home Hotel, The Ranch:* This is about 7 km from the central roundabout along the Sapele Road, on the outskirts of the city. There is a large signboard on the right of the road just past an Agip Petrol Station. Turn right and the hotel is on the left, about 0.5 km up the road. It has motel type accommodation with parking outside. Tel: (052) 244641 or 244394.

The *Saidi Centre* in Murtala Muhammad Way (between Sapele and Sakpoba roads) is Lebanese owned, and the restaurant has Lebanese and Chinese foods. Construction of a new accommodation was begun early in 1990. Tel: (052) 242125.

The *Emotan Hotel* is at 1 Central Road, in the GRA and has recently been refurbished. Tel: (052) 200130-2.

Other tourist sites

a. Abraka (see page 11).

b. The *Nana's Palace* at Koko on the coast is a worthwhile place to visit. Unfortunately, Koko recently received adverse publicity due to the dumping of toxic chemical waste in 1988. However, it has since been removed and there should no longer be any danger to visitors.

c. Source of the Ethiope River at Umutu near Abraka. There is a a spring, and a 'Juju' tree which is known for its large quantity of frogs.

d. *Okomu Forest Reserve.* The reserve is near Udo, west of Benin City. This reserve contains some of the last remaining rainforest in Nigeria, which is being preserved with the help of the Nigerian Conservation Foundation (NCF). It still has a herd of forest elephants and is home to the *white-faced monkey,* which is indigenous to Nigeria only. The forest is an excellent place to see birds and butterflies. Permission to visit the place is usually sought first from the NCF, 5, Mosley Road, Ikoyi, Lagos. Tel: (01) 686163 or 687385. There is a Guest House belonging to the African Timber and Plywood (AT & P) in the Reserve, but again, permission to use it must be obtained from AT & P or its parent company, the United Africa Company (UAC). Alternative accommodation, one hours journey away is at the *Okada Wonderland* which is signed to the left off the Benin expressway. Okada Wonderland has chalets with children's play parks, fish ponds and a Garden of Honour with cement statues of famous people. The accommodation is adequate.

e. Jakpa is a village on the Benin River not far from the coast, which has a history of early exploration and trade. Only approached by boat.

f. Old Warri: see Warri on page 41.

Erin - Ijesha Falls
General
Erin-Ijesha is a series of 7 waterfalls in Oyo State between Akure and Ilesha. The path to the bottom fall is only about 0.5 km from the car-park, and an easy walk. From there though, the path to the top is very steep. A fork to the right leads to the second fall from where there is a good view of the falls. The left fork

has smaller paths leading to different stages of the falls, but finally comes out onto the 'plateau'. This walk is only for the fit and agile! The area round the first fall is forested and cool and a pleasant place for a picnic, with benches to sit on, and easily accessible to the less agile.

Route

From Akure, the capital of Ondo State, take the Akure - Ilesha road. About 50 km from the outskirts of Akure there is a turning to the right marked 'To Erin-Oke'. Go through the village of Erin-Oke turning left at the T-junction just beyond the main road and proceed about 2 km into Erin-Ijesha along the main street. At the church and police station, take the right fork and almost immediately afterwards, turn right again where there is a sign to the falls. The car park is about 1 km further on, at the foot of the hills. It is at least a 4-hour drive from Lagos and it is best to make it a weekend trip, staying at Akure or Ibadan. There is an alternative route a few kilometres further along the main road, with a sign to the falls, but it is not obvious.

Hotels

The *Owena Motel* in Parliament Road, Akure is adequate. Coming from Ondo, turn left in Akure at the compulsory left sign and then right at the T-junction onto the dual carriageway. Proceed about $1\frac{1}{2}$ km and turn right at the 'Owena Motels Ltd' sign and left at the next junction by the NEPA building. Straight on, at the next roundabout and shortly after, turn right into the Motel. Tel: (034) 232560. A good alternative is the *Akure Plaza Hotel* Tel: 232075 or 231211.

Ibadan

General

Ibadan is said to be the largest city in Black Africa. It is the capital of Oyo State and is in the heart of Yorubaland. The University of Ibadan, abbreviated as UI, is the premier University in Nigeria. There are many seats of learning in Ibadan including a Teaching Hospital, the International Institute for Tropical Agriculture (IITA), the Cocoa Research Institute and the Federal Agricultural Research institute.

Tourist sites

a. The University and its bookshop. There is also a stall selling Adire cloth and some jewellery.

b. Ibadan Zoo - in the grounds of the University near the Zoology Department. The Zoo is small but children would enjoy it. The reptile house is of special interest.

c. There are several large markets in Ibadan, one of which, the Oje market, has a large section selling items for traditional medicines. *Ashoke* cloth, woven by men on narrow looms is also sold in the Ibadan market area.

d. The International Institute for Tropical Agriculture, (IITA), has a beautiful estate and many excellent facilities: a swimming pool, tennis courts, 9-hole golf course, squash court, a lake for fishing, excellent bird watching and a forest walk. However, it is not open to the public and permission must be obtained before visiting it.

Route

From Lagos there is a direct route via the Lagos - Ibadan expressway, but you can try taking a slower and more interesting journey up the old road to Ibadan from Lagos. The A1 through Ikorodu - Shagamu - Ajebo will give you more atmosphere than the busy expressway.

Hotels

The *Premier Hotel* is an option but many make Ibadan a day trip from Lagos. The Premier Hotel is an obvious landmark - a multi-storey white building on top of a hill not far from the Secretariat or Government buildings. It is also the largest hotel in Ibadan. There is an excellent view of the town from the hotel, but an alternative is the new (1988) *Kakanfo Inn* which is Indian-managed. It is just off the Ring-Road near the road to Abeokuta. Go up Adebiyi Street popularly called Joyce B road and it is on the left.

Idanre

General

The modern Yoruba town of Idanre in Ondo State is set in a valley surrounded by magnificent inselbergs rising to about 900 m. (Inselbergs are granite hills left standing above the surrounding countryside by the erosion of softer ground around them). Old Idanre is the original village, said to be 800 years old, which lies in a hanging valley reached by some 442 concrete steps. It was finally abandoned in 1933 although the Owa (Oba) still lives there for part of the year, and his palace is used for ceremonial occasions. Guides will take you up the steps to the village. There are resting places on the way up and at the top of the steps there are three rest houses (closed) but they have shady verandahs, and there is a magnificient view of the town from this point (best photographed with a wide-angled lens.) From there to the old village and the Owa's palace it is either a pleasant 15-minute walk along a shady path or a short scramble over the rocks. The Owa's palace has a fine courtyard with carved figures and doors. There is a shrine containing animal skulls and bones.

A further climb to a higher peak will bring you to various sacred sites, the mysterious mat and a magical footprint in the rock that is said to fit any foot that does not belong to a witch.

The Owa of Idanre traces the origin of his people through Oduduwa back to Egypt. The strange footprint is ascribed to that of Agbogun, the first son of Olofin, brother of Oduduwa who founded Idanre. (See page 24 on Ile-Ife for more about Oduduwa). It is possible also to climb to the meterological station at the top of the hill, which takes about another 40 minutes to get to the top. The first part is through forest, then a steep walk up the bare rock. There are magnificent views from the summit but this is definitely only for the very fit. (See Erin-Ijesha on page 19 for something else to do while in the area.) Allow $2\frac{1}{2}$ to 3 hours for the climb up and back to Old Idanre, with stops for refreshments. Local boys will guide you and carry your picnic things. Negotiate a price before engaging them. The price in 1990 was ₦20.

Route

The route from Lagos is along the Lekki dual carriageway to Epe, north to the Benin expressway, then turn right along the expressway to Ore, (or alternatively via Ikeja and Shagamu). At Ore, turn left (north) to Ondo. The road to Idanre is marked to the right about 23 km from Ondo on the Akure Road. There is also a road from Akure: turn south off the main road at the Post Office, and after passing the Oba's palace, take the first right, then first left, which is the Idanre road.

Hotels

The nearest place to stay is the *Owena Motel* Akure which is adequate. Coming from Ondo turn left in Akure at the compulsory left sign and then right at the T-junction. Turn right at the 'Owena Motels Ltd'. signed about $1\frac{1}{2}$ km along the road, and left at the NEPA building. Straight on, at the next roundabout and shortly afterwards, turn right into the motel.

Another good alternative is the Akure Plaza Hotel which the Nigerian Field Society uses. Go left off the dual carriageway (Adesina road) onto Oke Ijebu road. Go for a few kilometres to Plaza road. Follow the signs to the Plaza Hotel. It is well managed and helpful. Tel: (034) 232075 or 231211.

Ijebu-Ode Birikisu-Sungbo Shrine, Oke-Eri

General

The shrine, which is located near Ijebu-Ode (pronounced I-je-bo-de), at Oke-Eri, is the tomb of Birikisu, a noblewoman of note whom legend says became one of the wives of King Solomon, and therefore a 'Queen of Sheba'. It is said that Birikisu was such a powerful woman that she dug wells with the aid of needles. The shrine is a religious monument for muslims in Nigeria, and only *men* are allowed access to the tomb. It was said that a European woman once disregarded this advice and stepped onto the tomb. She is believed to have died in any accident soon afterwards. It is claimed that although the tomb is under the trees, no leaves fall on the tomb itself. In summary, the shrine is of great significance to muslims, but is not a tourist site as such. Permission to enter it must first be obtained from the caretaker, and you will be asked to remove your shoes. Ask for the caretaker in the village of Oke-Eri. In 1990 the charge was ₦10.

Route

Ijebu-Ode is an hour's journey from Lagos just off the Benin Expressway. Either take the Lekki Peninsula road to Epe and then north to Ijebu-Ode which is opposite the turn-off onto the expressway, or go north on the Ibadan expressway and thence to the Benin expressway. Go into Ijebu-Ode and take the Ibadan road. Shortly afterwards turn right to Oke-Eri just after a Felico filling station.

Hotels

The *Debasco Holiday Inn,* at Atiba near Ijebu-Ode on the road to Itoikin, was opened in May 1989. It has motel-style apartments, a conference hall, a disco and a tennis court. It is not connected to NEPA yet. So it uses a generator. The chalets have self-catering kitchens as there is no restaurant.

The Ooni of Ife

The Osun Shrine, Osogbo

The Anglican Cathedral, Lagos Island

Benin bronzes

View of the modern town of Idanre

A kob in Kainji Lake National Park, Borgu Sector

Fulani girl, Kwara State

Pied kingfisher *(Ceryle rudis)*

RANK XEROX

Document...

Electronic Typewriters

...Creation

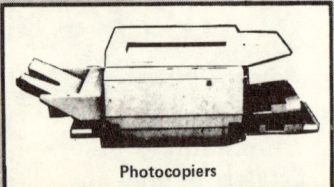
Photocopiers

...Duplication

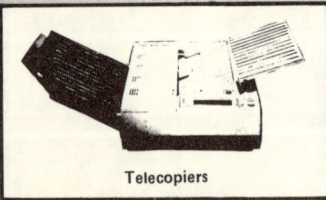
Telecopiers

...Transmission

Word Processors

...Retrieval

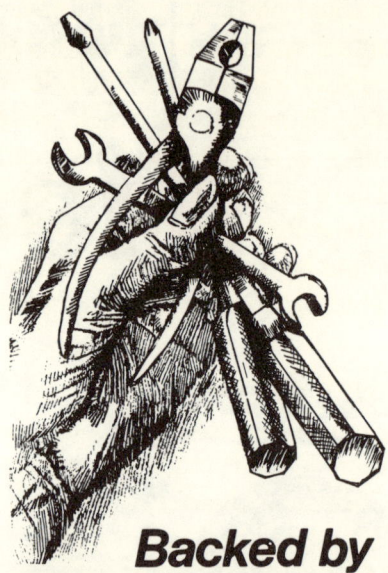

Backed by Xerox Service

Commitment to the needs of any business anywhere in the world is the essence of the services that Xerox products render.

Be it document creation, duplication, transmission or retrieval, there is always a Xerox product designed to give you the service you need.

Furthermore, all our products are backed by the Xerox people who give quality service that ensures unsurpassed document handling worldwide.

All enquiries to:
RANK XEROX NIGERIA LIMITED,
Block C, Plot 3, Fatai Atere Way.
Matori,Scheme, Oshodi,
P.M.B. 21314, Ikeja, Lagos.
Tel: 521500, 521614, 521532, 521543, 521552, 521562. Fax No 521569,.

RANK XEROX *—We taught the world to copy*

Ikogosi Warm Springs

General

The Ikogosi warm springs are at the village of Ikogosi (not marked on most maps) under an hour's drive from Akure. The actual springs are not of great significance, as the warm water bubbles out from a rock, forming a stream only a few inches deep. It meets with a cold water stream 100 m below. However, there is a swimming pool with warm water from the springs. There is also a very small 'Zoological Garden' beside the springs. These springs are only worth visiting if you are in the area, but it could be combined with a visit to the Ipole-Iloro water cataracts, which are 6 km north of Ikogosi.

Route

From Akure take the Ilesha road and after approximately 22 km there is a turning to the right at Igbara-Oke and Igbara-Odo by a CocaCola advert. Proceed for about $1\frac{1}{2}$ km into Igbara-Odo, turn left, after another 1 km turn right by a sign pointing to Ikogosi Motel. Drive 13 km to Igbara-Odo and turn left and immediately right into the village. At the T-junction, turn right and drive about 20 km to Ikogosi Ekiti. In this town, drive straight through the junction, past the motel, and the road to the Warm Springs is on the right at the fork.

Hotels

See Idanre on page 21 for directions to the Owena hotel at Akure. The tourist board have now built chalets at the Ikogosi warm springs. Warm water is supplied direct from the warm springs.

Ile-Ife

General

Ile-Ife, in Oyo State, is a unique city. To the Yorubas, it is the cradle of creation and civilisation and their legendary religous home. The legend says that it was at Ife that Oduduwa, sent form heaven by Olodumare, the Yoruba creator-God, established the first land upon the waters which then covered the earth, thus, becoming the founder of Ife. His sons spread to other parts of Yorubaland to create further kingdoms (see Idanre page 20).

Ile-Ife became a remarkable centre for arts, producing both terracotta figures and bronzes, dating from between the 12th and 15th centuries, and second only in fame to the Benin bronzes. Later, Ife declined in importance owing to the upheaval caused by the Fulani wars, and lost the art of bronze-making. The origins of Ife art still continue to baffle scholars, but it is thought that the bronzes were funeral effigies and the terracotta heads were used for the cult of ancestor worship and for shrine furniture. It was not until 1910 when a German, Leo Frobenius, took some of these figures to Germany, that this sophisticated African art-form was seen in Europe. The figures have been returned.

Tourist sites

a. *The Museum.* This is next to the Ooni's Palace, in the centre of the town, on Iremo Street. Here you can see the famous head of Olokun, the Sea Goddess, a representation of which is now the emblem of the University of Ife. The museum is small, but of great interest to those interested in African art, with its collection of terracotta heads, bronze figures and wood carvings. Some of the most significant artworks from Ile-Ife can also be seen in the National Museum in Lagos.

b. *The Ooni of Ife's Palace.* This is situated in the centre of the city on Iremo Street. The Ooni is the traditional ruler of Ile-Ife and according to Yoruba tradition, is descended from Oduduwa. It is possible to visit the Palace, but only if permission is sought first from the Ooni's secretary.

c. *Opa Oranyan (sometimes spelt Oranmiyan).* This is an engraved monolith about 5 m tall standing in a sacred grove south of the Palace off Iyekere Street, said to belong to the giant Oranyan. It was said to have been used in the defence of Ife against its enemies and said to have been turned to stone on the achievement of victory. Visitors may see and photograph the staff, but should not proceed further up the path to the shrine, as this might cause offence. In Ife there are several sacred groves with shrines but permission should be sought before visiting them, and a guide hired. Ask at the museum for information.

d. *University of Ife.* The Obafemi Awolowo University, as it is now called, was established in 1961 and moved to Ife in 1967. It is on the Ibadan road a few kilometres before Ile-Ife and has extensive grounds, with a park and a lake. The Institute of African Studies has been moved to the University Campus from the town, and has a gallery for contemporary Nigerian artists, but unfortunately it is not open at the weekend.

Route

From Lagos, Ile-Ife is best approached from Ibadan. Leave the expressway where the road is marked to Ife, and continue along the A12 to the town, which is 86 km from Ibadan.

Hotels

The *Hotel Diganga,* which is on the left hand side of the road coming from Ibadan, near the entrance to the University, is suitable for an overnight stay, but you can make it a day-trip from Lagos. The journey takes about 3 hours each way.

Ilorin

General

The ancient city of Ilorin is the capital of Kwara State. It is often described as the gateway between the northern and southern parts of the country because of its strategic location. It is a good base for visiting the surrounding area which has many tourist sites.

Tourist sites

a. *Alfa Alimi's Mosque* and residence - the mosque and residence were built in 1831. It was the first mosque in Ilorin. Alfa Alimi was a Fulani muslim scholar sent by the Sokoto Caliphate to preach Islam to the people of Ilorin. He also played a part in the disintegration of the Old Oyo Empire. Ask for the mosque, which is of historical value only and is in the back streets behind the Emir's palace which is beside the Central Mosque.

b. *Okuta Ilo Irin* (stone for sharpening metal tools) at Asaju's Compound at Idiape Quarters close to the Emir's palace. This is the stone on which one of the founders of Ilorin, known as Ojo Isekuse, used to sharpen his metal tools. The town derived its name from the use to which the stone was put. In the past, the stone was worshipped with sacrificial offerings, but this is no longer the case.

c. Dada pottery workshop in the Okelele quarter of Ilorin. It is one of the largest traditional pottery factories in the country.

There is also a calabash workshop at 91 Azeez Atta Road, opposite the Baptist Church in the Surulere district of Ilorin.

Other local tourist sites

a. *Esie Museum of stone figures* has approximately 1,000 soapstone figures of men and women sitting on stools. The stools are significant in having circular tops and bases joined by columns. There are some kneeling figures of both sexes with elaborate hair-styles and facial marks. Little is known about them except that they come from a very old civilisation. The museum houses the largest collection of stone images in Black Africa.

   Esie is near Oro on the Ilorin - Lokoja Road, a few kms past the town of Ajasse which is 42 km from Ilorin. At Oro, turn right off the main road into the town at a petrol station on the top of the hill. Turn left at the T-junction and take the right fork at the small square. Esie is the adjoining village across a small bridge, and the sign to the museum is just short of the village pointing to the right. It is about 2 km further, at the end of the road.

b. *Igbetti town.* This is the ancient city of the Oyo Obas. It is worth a visit if you are passing, but probably not worth a special expedition.

Route

To get to Ilorin take the expressway to Ibadan, continue north along the A1 through Oyo and Ogbomosho on a busy winding road to Ilorin. It is just over 300 km from Lagos so allow at least 4 to $4\frac{1}{2}$ hours.

Hotels

The *Kwara Hotel* is the recommended hotel in Ilorin, but it has not been well-maintained. The Chinese restaurant in the hotel serves excellent food. As you reach Ilorin, fork right at the AP garage. Turn right between the Total garage and the Fire Station, turn left at the next roundabout along the dual carriageway, and first right up the hill, Ahmadu Bello Avenue. Go straight on at the next roundabout and the Kwara Hotel is on the left after the government offices. Tel: (031) 221490. An alternative is the *Circular Hotel* in New Yidi Road. Tel: (031) 220845.

Iseyin

General
Iseyin is a good base for exploring this beautiful and unspoilt area of south-west Nigeria.

Tourist sites

a. Narrow loom weaving. There are a number of weavers around the town. They are to be found in compounds in the centre of the town, behind Iseyin market.

b. The Nigerian Tobacco Company (NTC) plant nursery. They have a large selection of garden plants available at competitive prices.

c. *Ogboro Inselberg.* Take the Shaki road and fork right at Ago-Are, then a left turn at Sepeteri. A guide (possibly carrying a long danegun) will take you up the inselberg having gained permission from the Oba of Ogboro (a bottle of spirits is the best *laisser-passer*). The climb is stiff. An old fortified village is at the summit. Baboons and monkeys may also be seen and on climbing down you go through defiles and bat-infested caves. Ogboro is about 100 km north of Iseyin along a poor road, so allow plenty of time for the journey.

d. *Ado-Awaiye Inselberg.* Take the Abeokuta road out of Iseyin, heading south-west. After about 26 km you will reach Ado-

Awaiye village. The Chief's permission to climb the inselberg should be obtained, and again a bottle of spirits may help. It is an energetic climb to the top, but a natural pool, curious depressions in the rock and the view are your rewards for the climb. From Lagos, approach via Abeokuta and take the Iseyin road. It is approximately 40 minutes from Abeokuta.

e. Oke-Iho Village. It is a pleasant unspoilt African village due west of Iseyin.

f. Shaki Town. This is an old city. May be worth seeing if you are going to Ogboro Inselberg and are making a day of it.

g. The Manor House. This is of interest to historians. It is on the top of the hill above the Catering Rest House. It was used by the British in colonial times as a residence and has superb views. The house was built on a grand scale with large rooms and an old fireplace. It is now used by the Oyo State Government.

Route

Iseyin is about 2 hours north-west of Ibadan and can be reached by going up the A1 Ibadan - Ilorin road. In Oyo town, turn left (west) and approximately 40 km further on, you will come to Iseyin.

Hotels

There is a catering rest house, *Trans-Nigeria Motels Ltd,* on the Abeokuta road, which is adequate. The Nigerian Tobacco Company has a comfortable and fully-equipped Rest House, but it is only possible to use it if you have permission from the Managing Director in Lagos. Remember, however, that company rest houses are for the employees of the company, and it is a privilege to be allowed to use them. The NTC Rest House is just past the Trans-Nigeria Motel, on the right. It is best to bring your own provisions for the steward to prepare.

Jebba

General

Jebba is one of the crossing points over the River Niger. It is where the A1 main road and the railway to the north cross the river. Jebba has an important railway station and is of historical importance.

Tourist sites

a. The remains of Baikie's boat, the 'Dayspring'. Baikie was sent to Africa to set up trading stations on the Niger but his boat, unfortunately foundered on some hidden rocks at Jebba on October 7th, 1857. The only remaining relics of the boat are metal items, including the propellor, so it is of limited interest. They are at the railway station beside an old steam engine which would be of interest to children and railway buffs.

b. The *Mungo Park and Lander monument,* a white obelisk, is on the island in the middle of the river which is spanned by the bridges. To reach it, drive off the northbound bridge to the right by the police station, turn underneath the bridge to the left and park. Follow the path on foot across the railway line and up to the monument, where you will get a spectacular view. For further reading on Mungo Park, Lander and Baikie, see *The Story of the Niger River - The Strong Brown God* by Sanche de Gramont.

c. The Jebba Hydro-electric Dam - on the River Niger, north of Jebba. You can see it from the bridge, but it may be possible to visit it, with permission from NEPA.

d. *Juju Rock.* This is an outstanding rocky island in the River Niger which can also be clearly seen from the bridge. It is here that some extraordinary Nupe bronze figures, dating from the

15th century, were discovered. The nine Toesede bronzes, from here and from the village of Tada, are the largest cast bronzes ever found in Africa, and six are now in the National Museum, Lagos. they have clear affinities with early Ife and Benin bronze-work.

Route

Lagos - Ibadan - Oyo - Ogbomosho - Ilorin bypass - Jebba. To take the Ilorin bypass, turn left (west) at a junction between Ogbomosho and Ilorin, signed to Jebba.

Hotels

The *National Paper Mills Guest House* at Jebba is signed to the left just before the bridge, coming from the south. Follow the road up the hill to the guardpost of the paper mills compound and ask for directions. However, it is not open on Sundays and public holidays.

Kainji Dam/Borgu Game Reserve

General

The Lake Kainji National park consists of 2 separate parts: the Zurgurma Sector to the south-east in Niger State whose chalets, as at the time of writing, were still under construction, and the Borgu Game Reserve, west of Lake Kainji and the Dam, which already has accommodation for visitors.

Tourist sites

a. *Kainji Dam.* In 1958, Balfour Beatty, a British Company, was commissioned to look into the feasibility of a dam on the Niger. In 1964, the dam was started. The project was estimated to cost about £144 million, but ended up nearer £173 million. The dam itself was built by the Italians with British, Austrian, Swedish and Italian electrical equipment. There are 4 sections to the dam. The principal section is concrete, 5,486 m long with a height of 65.5 m. The generators were designed to produce 880 mega watts of power. Unfortunately, it has not succeeded in achieving this for many reasons, including lack of water. The artificial lake covers Old Bussa where Mungo Park, the explorer, was said to have come to grief in 1805. But the scene of the accident is no longer visible. The lake is 136 km long. Tours of the dam are available on request from the Nigeria Electric Power Authority (NEPA). Boat trips on the lake can be arranged by the Borgu Game Reserve office at Wawa. However, it is expensive unless there are several visitors to share the cost, and the road to the embarkation point is not good. Fishing is allowed on the lake.

b. *Borgu Sector of Lake Kainji National Park.* The park was set up as a Federal Game Reserve in 1979. It is 950 sq km and is one of the largest in West Africa. The area was uninhabited and the idea for the reserve was conceived in 1960. It is in the northern guinea vegetation zone which is characterised by tall grasses and savanna woodland. The reserve still has a reasonable animal population including antelope (kob), lion, hippopotamus, buffalo, roan antelope, jackal, baboon, monkey and crocodile but the elephants appear to have left the reserve. The reserve is open from December to June and the best time to visit is at the end of the dry season when the grass has died down and the animals have moved closer to the water. There is always the risk of harmattan from December to mid-February but this should not put you off.

The best times for game viewing are in the early morning or evening, and trips can be arranged from 6.00 am either in park vehicles or your own vehicle. Bird life is abundant, especially near the river, but animals are less often seen than at Yankari and game reserves in East Africa.

Visitors should call at the Wawa Game Warden's office (18 km from New Bussa) to be briefed and to book a game guide.

The entrance to the reserve is approximately 30 km from Wawa along a laterite road, and the Oli River Camp is a further 50 km from the entrance.

c. *Wildlife Trophies Museum/Restaurant.* This is at the office premises at Wawa. The museum is small but may be worth a visit, especially for children. The restaurant serves local food, soft-drinks and beer. Game reserve T-shirts are on sale in the shop.

d. *Uwuru Rapids.* The Uwuru Rapids were on the Niger River south of the dam, but are now covered by water as a result of the Jebba Dam.

Other tourist sites

You may wish to explore further north from Wawa towards Yelwa and the Niger ferry to the north of the Kainji Lake. There are various Kamberi villages along the route, which have interesting markets on different days of the week. The road is laterite and badly corrugated.

Route

The route from Lagos is Ibadan - Ilorin bypass (turn left at the sign to Jebba between Ogbomosho and Ilorin) - Jebba - Mokwa. At Mokwa, turn left (west) to Kainji and New Bussa just before you reach the town. The distance from Lagos to New Bussa, where there is a motel, is about 543 km. This can be done in a day, but some may prefer to break their journey en route. If you are staying at the Oli River Camp, (which is approximately 100 km further), take the second turning right off the roundabout at New Bussa, heading north-west, to Wawa (18 km). Turn left when you reach the T-junction and the game reserve office is about 100 m on the right. Here you can pick up a guide for the 80 km to the camp, which is all on untarred roads and can take up to 2 hours. Petrol can be obtained from Oli River Camp, but it would be wise to have a reserve supply.

Hotels

At New Bussa the *Kainji Motel* is the recommended accommodation. It has 4 VIP suites and 40 double rooms. The motel is adequate but there is no choice of food. It is not expensive but be prepared for fairly basic living. If you have children, it would be wise to take some of their favourite food to supplement. The swimming pool was not in use on our visit. From the roundabout turn right, then take the third large turning on the left (3 km). Continue along this road until it curves to the right, and the Kainji Motel is on your right.

The Oli River Lodge inside the reserve is only open from December to June. It provides reasonable accommodation and a simple restaurant, and is a good base inside the park from which to go game viewing. The rooms have airconditioners but the generator is only used at night. As it is on the Oli River there is a good bird-watching area around the camp. However, take some protection against the tsetse flies.

Lokoja

General

Lokoja, in Kwara State, is an historic town, and due to its position at the confluence of the 2 great rivers, the Niger and the Benue, it became the headquarters of the Royal Niger Company in the 19th century. Lord Lugard, who brought the north of Nigeria under British control, had his quarters at Lokoja, which are still standing. These were pre-fabricated buildings and no nails were used in their construction. Bishop Samuel Ajayi Crowther, the first African bishop in Nigeria, also lived in Lokoja. Another 'first' was the founding of Holy Trinity School, the earliest primary school in the country. There is reputed to be an 'Iron of Liberty' - the iron which slaves could touch to regain their freedom, inside the compound of this school. The graveyard con-

ACCESS BANK
NIGERIA LIMITED

Your Path to excellent international banking

When you need the services of a Nigerian bank for your international business transactions, you can be assured that ACCESS BANK will meet your highest expectations in terms of prompt, efficient and convenient services.

Because at ACCESS BANK, our well-trained staff are very versatile in international banking methods...with vast experience in:

FOREIGN EXCHANGE TRANSACTIONS
- Letters of Credit
- Bills for Collection
- Open Account Settlement

EXPORT TRADE AND FINANCING
- Export Credit
- Export Advisory Services
- Rediscounting and Refinancing Facility
- Export Stimulation Loan

DOMICILIARY ACCOUNT OPERATIONS
(With attractive interest)
We are supported by reputable correspondence worldwide.

ACCESS BANK –Your access to excellent banking

4, Burma Road, Apapa, P. O. Box 4560, Lagos. Tel: 804310-4, 875834

The greatest force in Express Delivery Service, Worldwide.

IMNL, Nigeria's No.1 Courier Company and United Parcel Service (U.P.S), the world's No.1 Courier Company have come together to generate a new force in Express Delivery Service.

IMNL, with over a decade of experience, offer the widest range of services, fast and safe ... including Domestic and International document and parcel express, Sameday Express and Heavyweight Express.

UPS, nearly a century old, with a staff strength of over 237,000, specially trained to handle operations in over 200 countries in the world.

With a fleet of 363 aircraft and over 116,000 vehicles, UPS handles over 11 million parcels a day.

Now, with our well proven and enviable record in Express Delivery Services, we cover the world-effectively.

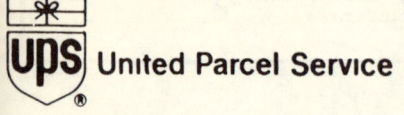

Plot 16, Cworonshoki Expressway, Gbagada Industrial Estate, P.O. Box 2780, Ikeja, Lagos, Nigeria Tel: 01-824202, 824214, 824218. Telex: 26672 (IMNL NG.) Fax No.: 824

Wellcome Nigeria Limited...

...investing for improved health in the nation

Wellcome Nigeria Limited - incorporated in 1962 - was one of the first pharmaceutical companies to set up manufacturing facilities in Nigeria when it opened its Ikeja factory in 1966 with the controlling shares owned by The Wellcome Foundation Limited, London.

In 1974 the Foundation donated one-third of its shareholding to a Nigerian trust, Wellcome Nigeria Fund, run independently by a group of eminent Nigerians in the medical and allied professions, with the objective of utilising the profits it receives from Wellcome Nigeria Limited in the support of medical and allied research in Nigeria.

With the policy of identifying with the nation's aspirations, Wellcome Nigeria Limited has made tremendous investments in pharmaceutical manufacturing facilities - modern equipment, structure and manpower development - and built up a reputation for the local manufacture and marketing of pharmaceutical products of the highest international standards.

More than 99% of Wellcome's employees are Nigerians, most of them being high calibre professionals in the pharmaceutical and allied fields whose skills are continuously being improved by way of further training.

As a member of the Wellcome Group, Wellcome Nigeria Limited benefits from its sound research activities and constantly invests these results for improved health in this nation.

WELLCOME NIGERIA LIMITED
Oba Akran Avenue,
P.M.B. 21099, Ikeja

Wellcome
-FOR A HEALTHIER, HAPPIER LIFE.

ICL/WL 262

7up Money Spinner

₦5,000,000

230,000 winners

Drink a bottle of **7up**, **PEPSI**, **MIRINDA** or **TEEM** Lemonade and look under the crown for the winning symbols, as shown.

Take your winning crowns to any of our salestrucks, depots, plants or offices and cash your money on the spot.

₦100			▶	₦100
₦50			▶	₦50
₦20			▶	₦20
₦10			▶	₦10
Free Drink			▶	Free Drink

7up — The difference is clear

tains the graves of some of the Northern Emirs exiled to Lokoja after Lord Lugard's campaign, and several British servicemen and colonial officers. There is a fine memorial to the Nigerian soldiers who were killed in the two world wars. Lokoja is perhaps of more interest to the historian rather than the tourist, but there is a magnificent view of the confluence of the 2 rivers from the top of Mount Patti, behind the town. Unfortunately, many of the historical places are not obvious and to find them needs determination and patience. Possibly one of the older citizens might be persuaded to act as a guide.

Route

From Lagos, the most direct route is via the Benin expressway to Ore, then turn left and go through Ondo, Akure and a few kilometres past the Owo bypass (on the Ifon road), take a turning to the left along a new road at Ipele which goes directly to Kabba and then on to Lokoja. An alternative route is through Benin City and Auchi.

Hotels

There is a catering Rest House in Lokoja, but, unfortunately, it has seen better days.

Offa

This is a small town 50 km south of Ilorin, near Esie, and might be worth a visit if you are going to the Museum at Esie. The Olofa of Offa has a traditional palace here and the late Olofas have a tomb in the town. The Onimoka Shrine and the Afelele Lake may also be of interest. The Onimoko Yam Festival is held around July/August and is an exciting festival featuring a wrestling combat between the traditional ruler and his second-in-command, the ceremonial cutting of the new yam, and cultural dancing.

Route

From Ilorin take the Lokoja road to Ajasse and then turn right (south) towards Offa, or approach from Oshogbo in the south, but either way some of the road was in poor condition in 1990.

Okomu Forest Reserve (See Benin City on page 14)

Omo Forest

General

This is the Ogun State Forestry Plantation Project north of the Benin expressway, about 2 hours journey from Lagos. It can only be entered with permission from the manager of the project, Office J4, Box 2068, Ijebu-Ode. It is mentioned in this guide as it is of special interest to naturalists and ornithologists. There are bird-watching sites, primary forest (rapidly being cut down), a bailey bridge over the Sasa river and a pleasant lake with a boathouse. The Forestry Project has chalets which can be hired on application and there is a club house with a wide verandah for picnics, but it has no staff or facilities. The Nigerian Field Society (NFS) sometimes organises trips to this forest, and it would be best to contact a member to guide you, but remember to obtain permission first.

Route

From Lagos take the road along the Lekki Peninsula to Epe, and then to Ijebu-Ode. Turn right onto the Benin expressway and continue for approximately 30 km until you see a wide laterite road on your left at the top of a hill. (Coming from the Benin direction, turn right near the 'Shagamu 78 km' post). Continue on the road, through 2 barriers and turn right to the lake past the staff houses. If you should drive further into the forest, use a compass and take a note of your route, as it is easy to get lost. All roads look the same inside the forest! It is better to be guided on the first occasion. (From Ikeja or mainland Lagos, take the Ibadan expressway to Shagamu and turn right onto the Benin Expressway. The turn-off is 30 km past the Fari petrol station at Ijebu-Ode).

Oshogbo

General

Oshogbo was the site of the great battle between the Fulani invaders from the north and the Yoruba armies of the south in 1838-9, in which the Fulani were decisively defeated. Legend gives much credit for their defeat to the river goddess, Osun, who is supposed to live in the river near the shrine. An Austrian-born artist, Suzanne Wenger, has done much to revive the cult of Osun in recent years, and with the help of Yoruba artists, has created strange and interesting cement sculptures and carvings. There is an extensive area to visit in a peaceful forest setting. The shrine itself is near the river, and from the old iron bridge nearby there is a pleasant view of the river. There are other sacred areas across the road with dramatic sculptures, including one depicting elephants and another a market. There are guides who will show you round for a small charge. You may also be asked to contribute money at the shrine itself. Suzanne Wenger still lives in Oshogbo (1990) and her house is also decorated with sculptures. There is a small craft shop in her house, which is in the centre of the town. From the green and red mosque turn left at the 'Marlboro' traffic box and then first right. Her house is on the left going down the hill.

Oshogbo town is famous for its arts and crafts: painting, wood carving, decorated calabashes and batik dyeing. The artist, Twin Seven Seven, one of the best-known artists of Oshogbo, and Nikki Olanyi, who has exhibited her batiks in London and New York, both live on the old Ede road. Twin Seven Seven, who is also a musician, lives opposite the Grammar School, and Nikki lives nearer Ede. It is probably best to visit Oshogbo as part of a tour with the Nigerian Field Society or with some other cultural societies in order to have a guided tour of the various art centres, Suzanne Wenger's house and St Joseph's Workshop. The latter is some kilometres north of Oshogbo, and produces excellent wood carvings. However, individuals or small parties will enjoy the visit too.

Route
From Lagos, take the expressway to Ibadan and then take the Ife road signed off the expressway (A122) to Gbongan (about 50 km). Turn north-east (signed to the Oshogbo Steel Works) opposite an Agip petrol station, to Oshogbo. In Oshogbo, there is a sign to the right leading to the Osun (pronounced Oshun) shrine. Continue up the road until you reach a T-junction, turn right and continue to the large green and red Central Mosque. Turn right again and carry on for 2 km until you reach the shrine. This is indicated by the sculptures beside the road, and the entrance to the shrine is on the left beside the small car park.

Hotels
The *Osun Presidential Hotel,* Old Ikirun Road, (Tel: 035-232399) is a satisfactory stopover if you wish to stay in Oshogbo, but Ibadan is only an hour's journey away. You can make it a day trip from Lagos if you start early in the morning, as the journey takes 3 hours each way.

Owo

General
Owo is an old Yoruba town which was originally walled. It is now notable for its small, but interesting, collection of Yoruba sculp-

tures in the local museum in front of the Olowo's palace. These were excavated in 1971. The Olowo's palace is the largest in Yoruba-land, covering a 99 hectre piece of land to the west of the town. There are over 100 ancient courtyards of which 17 are still reasonably intact.

Route

Lagos - Benin expressway to Ore, turn left to Ondo and Akure. Owo is less than 1 hour's drive east from Akure. Turn right at the turning from the main Akure road into the centre of the town and right again up a small slope. The Olowo's palace is on the right with ample parking space. Ask, if there is any doubt. Everyone knows the Olowo's palace.

Hotels

There is no suitable hotel. It is better to stay at the *Owena Motel* or *Akure Plaza* in Akure. For directions to the motel, see Erin-Ijesha on page 18.

Owu Falls (sometimes called the Ore Falls)

General

Owu Falls in Kwara State is the highest and most spectacular natural waterfall in West Africa. Naturally, it is at its most spectacular in the wet season. The fall cascades 100 m down an escarpment with rocky outcrops, to a pool of ice-cold water below. The path leads right to the pool alongside a tree-lined stream. The views en route to the town of Owa Kajola are scenic and the escarpment is a very impressive sight.

Route

The falls are about 95 km from Ilorin. At Ilorin take the Lokoja road (A123) for about 61 km until you reach the village of Oke-Inigbin (shortly before Omu-Aran), where the falls are signed to the left (north). Take a laterite road for 11 km to Isanlu-Isin, turn left at the T-junction, and continue to the village of Owa Kajola (28 km), turning left at the sign to the falls near a church. At the end of the road, follow the track on foot for about

2 km. (The distance from the main road is about 33 km in all.) In April 1990, a bulldozer was enlarging the track, and there were plans to tar the road, but it was still necessary to ford a stream on the road beyond Owa Kajola which may be impassable in the wet season until it is bridged.

Hotels

See Ilorin on page 27 for information on hotels.

Pategi

Pategi is on the River Niger in Kwara State, and is known for its regattas when the Nupe people from Pategi and Bida have fishing, swimming and canoeing competitions on the river. The long canoes are manned by many paddlers, and it is a spectacular sight. The date of the festival is not fixed. It is necessary to make enquiries from the local area or go to the Kwara State Liaison Office in Victoria Island, Lagos, for information. Pategi is also known for the carving of wooden doors. It is suggested that Ilorin is used as a base.

Route

From Ilorin, take the Lokoja road until you reach Egbe. From there it is approximately 60 km to the north, much of it along a rough laterite road which could be difficult to negotiate in the wet season.

Sapele, Koko and Jakpa

a. Sapele

This is an old trading post and port on the confluence of the Ethiope and Jamieson rivers where they become the Benin River. The African Timber and Plywood Company (AT & P) is based here with a large sawmill and timber processing plant. The name 'Sapele' itself has been given to a type of hardwood exported from this region. The town of Sapele is not of great note except for some rather ornate old houses, but if you can hire a boat, a trip up the Jamieson River is a very pleasant outing. The AT & P Company, which is a subsiduary of the United Africa Company (UAC) has a guest house there, which can be used with their permission. If you cannot hire a boat, it is possible to get to the Jamieson River at Sapoba by car, where there is a pleasant picnic spot. The river upstream from Sapoba is beautifully clear, and suitable for swimming, although the water is surprisingly cold.

b. Koko

Koko received much publicity in 1988 owing to the dumping of toxic waste there. However, this has now been removed and the area is considered safe to visit. The traditional ruler has a palace in Koko, called the Nana's Palace.

c. Jakpa

This is an old trading post almost at the estuary of the Benin river which has an old canon, glass bottles and other relics of the past. The only way to reach it is to go by boat from Sapele down the Benin River. The banks of the river are covered in mangrove, very much a feature of the delta region of Nigeria.

Warri and Patani

Warri

Warri is one of the major oil ports of the delta region of Nigeria. It has a large refinery and an airfield. The old town is worth a visit if you are in Warri. There are many oil fields, oil pipelines and oil installations in the area. The area can easily be identified from the flaring of excess gas in huge jets of flame.

Route

From Benin City take the Sapele road from the central roundabout and Warri is approximately 100 km to the south.

Hotels

The *Palm Grove Motel*, Upper Erejuwa Road, is adequate for an overnight stay.

Patani

Patani is on the bank of the River Forcardos, one of the major branches of the Niger River after it divides into several rivers in the delta region. It is on the main Warri-Port Harcourt road and there is a motel on the bank of the river which, although little used, can make a useful picnic spot on a journey. The bar serves cold drinks and for a small charge you can eat your picnic in pleasant surroundings. It could be used as an overnight stop as it has chalets. There are pleasant views of the river from the motel.

Route to the Motel

From Warri take the Port Harcourt road, and approximately 2 km before the large bridge at Patani there is a small road to the right. Continue along this road (roughly parallel with the main road) for 2 km until you reach a T-junction near the river. Turn right and the motel is on the left through some large metal gates. It has a pleasant view of the river traffic (the local ferries and fishermen), and an imposing bridge over the River Forcardos.

3

South-East

Introduction

General

South-east Nigeria covers the area bordered by the River Niger in the west, the River Benue in the north, the border with Cameroon in the east and the Gulf of Guinea/Bight of Benin to the south. Much of the southern area consists of the delta region of the River Niger and its tributaries, with large areas of mangrove and swamps. In the east the country is mountainous and has the Oban Hills, and the Obudu and Mambilla Plateaux. Plateaux are

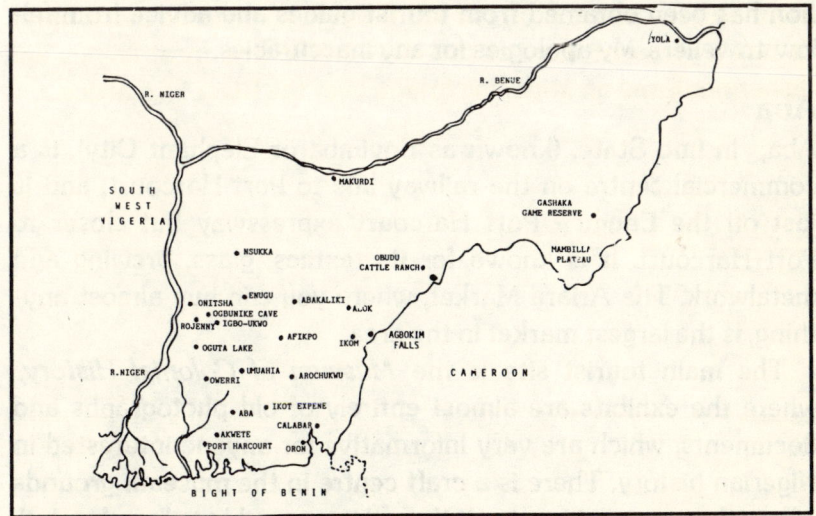

features of this area, but the south-east also includes the Cross River and the historical port of Calabar.

The South-east is the region of the oil industry which is of great economic importance to Nigeria. Between the River Niger and the Cross River valley there is an escarpment running north from Okigwe through Awgu and Udi to Nsukka and as far as the Benue valley, where some attractive hilly country can be seen.

This area has many different ethnic groups apart from the Igbo, the major group, whose culture dates back several centuries. It is very much the land of the masks, masquerades *(mmanwu),* shrines and wood carvings, examples of which can be seen in the museums. The region has a strong Christian background as a result of the many missionaries who came to this part of the country from 1857 and founded a large number of schools. Festivals are very much a feature of this area, including the Christmas and New Year festivals held at most towns and villages. The New yam festivals are not held on the same day each year, so the dates must be checked locally.

Only the major tourist sites are covered, so it is always worth consulting the local people for further information. The majority of the sites have been visited by the author, but some information has been obtained from tourist guides and advice from fellow-travellers. My apologies for any inaccuracies.

Aba

Aba, in Imo State, (known as Enyimba or Elephant City), is a commercial centre on the railway line to Port Harcourt, and is just off the Enugu - Port Harcourt expressway but closer to Port Harcourt. It is known for its textiles, glass, brewing and metalwork. The Ariara Market, where you can buy almost anything, is the largest market in the area.

The main tourist site is the *Museum of Colonial History,* where the exhibits are almost entirely of old photographs and documents, which are very informative for anyone interested in Nigerian history. There is a craft centre in the museum grounds where they weave Akwete cloth, and it is possible to buy the cloth here, but of course, there is a better selection in the town of Akwete itself (see page 46). Aba was a garrison town and a District headquarters in the colonial times, and the museum is in an old colonial building on the outskirts of the town on the Ikot-Ekpene road, A342. It is on the right of the road before crossing the Aba River bridge, and is worth a visit if you are passing that way. The museum is open from 9.00 am to 6.00 am daily.

Abakaliki

Abakaliki is in Anambra State, east of Enugu, on the A343 road to Ogoja, but at the time of writing the road was badly potholed. For those interested in Nigerian cloth, there is a good cloth market there, where local 'tie and dye' cloth, dyed in indigo, which is similar to Adire cloth, is sold.

Afikpo - Ishiagu Pottery

Afikpo is in the north-east corner of Imo State close to the Cross River, and is known for its pottery and mask making. On the Afikpo road from Okigwe is the Afikpo Road Railway halt (station), and near here you can usually purchase Ishiagu pottery, on both sides of the Uturu - Afikpo road. Ishiagu itself is about 3km away down a local road. The clay pots made in the area by the women are well designed and beautifully shaped, many decorated with figures and elaborate handles. Most of the pots have lids. Afikpo is also a traditional centre for mask making, which is done in the old central part of the town. Afikpo is an attractive hilly country, which is well worth a visit in its own right. For the nearest good accommodation, see Enugu (page 51).

Agbokim Waterfalls

Agbokim Waterfalls is a very attractive tourist spot near Ikom in Cross River State, close to the Cameroon border. It is an impressive sight, even in late December. So it would be magnificent in the wet season. It is less than 30 km from Ikom on a good tarred road, and would make an excellent picnic spot if you are travelling in the area, as you can drive right to the falls which are situated in pleasant forest surroundings. It is possible to climb down a rough path to the bottom of the valley where you can see underneath the overhang of the falls. There are no facilities at Agbokim, but Ikom has a motel overlooking the Cross River which is suitable for an overnight stop, called the *Metro Hotel*.

Route

From Ikom take the road towards the Cameroon border, but take the first turning left after about $1\frac{1}{2}$ km. Continue on this road for approximately 25km, to the end of the road, through a village. The road ends in a circular 'roundabout' right beside the falls; so it is easy to find. The road is tarred and in good condition.

Akwete Textile Centre

Akwete is a town in Imo State north-east of the Port Harcourt-Enugu expressway. It is well-known for its brightly coloured cloth, which is woven by the women on a broad wooden loom about $1\frac{1}{2}$ m wide. The place is worth a visit if you are near Port Harcourt and interested in weaving. For accommodation, see page 63, on Port Harcourt.

Route

From Port Harcourt, take the expressway towards Enugu, and after about 45 km there is a turning to the right between a Texaco petrol station and an AP petrol station, where there is a sign pointing to the Akwete Rubber Research Institute (the sign is not very obvious). Continue along this winding road past the research institute, until you reach the village of Akwete. The weaving centre is in a new building on the right of the road, about 300 m past the large and well-built church.

Alok Stone Monoliths

There are a number of carved stone monoliths in Cross River State, but the best are around Alok, which is a small village about one hour north of Ikom on the Ogoja road. The village is not marked. So the only way to find it is to ask along the road. It is on the left, some distance past an army camp which is 22 km from Ikom. The caretaker of the stones is most enthusiastic, and he will show you the monoliths in the village, (pictured in Peter Holmes's book, *Nigeria, Giant of Africa*), the sacred grove of 'cot-cot' trees just outside the village where sacrifices are made, and a circle of stones to the north of the village further along the main road. This latter area is controlled by the Department of Antiquities based at the National Museum in Lagos, where there are further examples of the monoliths on the lawn in front of the main building. The caretaker of the stones at Alok is SE Akong, and can be reached through Post Office Box 538, Ikom.

The sculptured granite stones represent human figures and are considered sacred by the local people. Their age is not known but the earliest may date from the 16th century. They represent an advanced form of stone-carving, as the granite is a hard crystalline rock, requiring a great deal of labour to produce such precise work. Other stones are to be found in the area, some in deep forest. Another site is in a grove at the roadside near Meghawe, a little beyond the mile 111 sign on the Enugu - Ogoja - Gboko road. An annual festival is held there at the end of the dry season.

Hotels

There is a motel called the *Metro* at Ikom, overlooking the Cross River, to the south-west of the town, which is suitable for an overnight stop.

Arochukwu Shrine (The Long Juju)

The cave of the Oracle of the Long Juju is at Arochukwu in the south-east corner of Imo State, due south of Ohafia. The shrine is decorated with juju objects and has a long metal pipe through which the gods were said to speak. The Long Juju was said to have divine knowledge and was thought to know everything that was happening. A chief priest administered the shrine, assisted by agents who travelled far and wide in disguise, seeking out disputes. Once a dispute was encountered, the antagonists were persuaded to consult the Long Juju. The guilty party was thought to be devoured by the juju, but in reality it was a ruse as some were smuggled out of a back entrance and sold into slavery.

Although it was destroyed in the colonial days, it has been restored and the Long Juju is still respected by some of the local people. The nearest suitable accommodation is at Owerri or Port Harcourt (see pages 62 and 63). Unless you are especially interested in traditional religion, it is probably not worth a special visit, though it is of photographic interest with permission.

Calabar

General

Calabar is well worth a visit, as it is an attractive city on the bank of the Calabar River near its junction with the Cross River and has a long history as the port of the eastern region of Nigeria, first visited by the Portuguese at the end of the 15th Century. It became the administrative headquarters of the Oil Rivers Protectorate, the British protectorate of Southern Nigeria. (The oil in this case was palm oil, for which the region was an important trading centre). The history of Calabar is bound with the history of the Efik ethnic group, of which the Obong of Calabar is the traditional ruler. The people trace their ancestory back to Babylon before the time of Christ. Calabar is also the centre from which many missionaries ventured forth in the 19th and 20th centuries, including Mary Slessor who arrived in Calabar in 1875.

Kalabari Masquerade, Bakana Island

Agbokim Falls near Ikom

The church at Akwete

Stone monoliths at Alok near Ikom

Kwa Falls, near Calabar

Ikot Ekpene tourist market

Obudu Cattle Ranch

The National War Museum, Umuahia

Her position was unique in this area. In spite of coming from the slums of Dundee in Scotland, she made such an impression that she became a Vice Consul at Okoyong, and the President of the Native Court. The Okoyong people called her 'The White Queen'.

Calabar is the capital of Cross River State and has good road and river communications into the hinterland. The town is served by an airport, linking it with Lagos and other parts of the country.

Tourist sites

a. *The National Museum.* This is in the old Residency building. The building was pre-fabricated and shipped from Britain and erected on the top of Consular Hill in 1884. The hill later became known as the Government Hill. The museum is well worth a visit just to see an old colonial building of such style on a site with superb views of Calabar and the Calabar River. The museum traces the history of Calabar and the surrounding area, and is extremely well-set out. A guidebook is on sale, which is a valuable guide to the museum and a useful history book as well.

b. *Mary Slessor's Cottage.* Mary Slessor's cottage is at Ekenge across the river from Calabar, so a boat trip is required. It is suggested that only keen historians make such an expedition. Mary Slessor's gravestone is in a graveyard in Enendem Street in Calabar, although it is rather neglected. It is on a hill at the south-west end of the town with a beautiful view overlooking the river. Her memorial, which was recently erected, is nearby.

Other tourist Sites Outside Calabar
Oban Hills and Kwa Falls

This is a scenic area that is well worth seeing on a day trip from Calabar. The falls are approximately 39 km from Calabar on the road towards Oban, at Aningeje, and you can drive right to the top of the falls where there is a bar, (not always open). The waterfall is in a deep valley with beautiful forest surroundings, and you can walk down the 150 or so steps to the river below. It is possible to walk upstream to the falls where there are deep pools, by scrambling over the rocks, but do remember to take insect repellant as the sandflies are vicious. Our climb down was rewarded by the sight of a giant kingfisher and a pair of mountain wagtails.

There are also tea plantations in this area and recently a Forest Reserve was opened. If you wish to visit this reserve, please contact a member of the Nigerian Conservation Foundation (NFC) in Lagos, 5, Moseley Road, Ikoyi, Tel: (01) 686163/687385.

Route

A direct route is Lagos - Benin City - Onitsha - Owerri - Aba - Ikot - Ekpene - Calabar. It is a day journey to Calabar but good stopping-off points would be either the Oguta Lake (see page 61) or the Concorde Hotel in Owerri, (see page 63). To get to the Oban Hills and Kwa Falls starting from the Metropolitan Hotel in Calabar, take the main dual carriageway north for about 2 1/2 km, then turn right at the traffic lights between the Mobil and National petrol stations onto the Oban road. At the village of Aningeje, (about 34 km), go past the market and turn left at the sign which says 'Welcome to Palm Plantation Ltd, Kwa Falls Estate'. A laterite road leads through the oil palm estate for about 3 km to the falls. At a place where the road forks, there is a sign pointing right in the direction of the falls.

Hotels

Calabar has no 5-star hotels, but the recommended hotel is the *Metropolitan* which is on the left of the dual carriageway as you enter Calabar. The telephone number is (087) 220911/2. An alternative is the *Paradise Hotel* at 86/88 Atekong Drive. Tel:

(087) 225726. To get there, turn left off the dual carriageway down Atekong Drive, opposite the Ministry of Justice which can be seen on the right of the road just before reaching the Metropolitan Hotel.

Enugu

General

Enugu is the capital of Anambra State, one of the two Igbo states famed for the friendliness of its people and is the centre of the Nigeria coal industry, but do not let this put you off. It is situated in attractive hilly country and is a well laid-out city with wide roads and expressways and main roads leading to the north, south, east and west. It is very much a centre of communications with an airport and the railway to Port Harcourt, which passes through the city. It has some faculties of the University of Nigeria located in the city. It also boasts of one of the best hotels in Nigeria, as at the date of this guide (1990) the Nike Lake Hotel.

Tourist sites

The main places of interest are:
a. *Enugu National Museum* (closed in 1989 but to be re-opened and relocated on the Abakaliki Road).
b. Cultural Division Art Gallery, 7 Onitsha Road.

Route

The direct route is Lagos - Benin City - Onitsha - Enugu expressway and takes about 7 hours. The expressway between Onitsha and Enugu was recently repaired and is, in good condition.

Hotels

The best hotel is the excellent *Nike Lake Hotel* which is to the north-east of Enugu. Travelling east on the dual carriageway you will see it signed to the left at the Penoks petrol station, and it is well-signed from there on. It is a new hotel (built in 1988) in attractive surroundings with good management. There is a swimming pool and several tennis courts, and as the name implies, there is a small lake beside the hotel, with two rowing-boats for use by guests. Tel: (042) 337000. Telex 51448 NIKTEL EN ENG.

The other main hotel in Enugu is the *Presidential,* on Presidential Road, which has recently undergone a change of management. It is cheaper than the Nike Lake, but does not have the same facilities. Tel: (042) 337472.

Gashaka-Gumti Game Reserve

This is a vast expanse of spectacular wilderness, (6,000 km), in the south-east corner of Gongola State, adjoining the Mambilla Plateau. Much of the reserve is mountainous, ranging from 457.2 - 2407 m, and Nigeria's highest mountain, Chapal Waddi (2,407 m) is in the reserve. It is the most ecologically diverse conservation area in the country and contains areas of guinea savanna, gallery forest, moist forest, and both montane forest and grassland. Many rivers flow through the reserve, including the Taraba, a major tributary of the River Benue. There is a wide variety of animal life including buffalo, hartebeest, roan antelope, chimpanzee, colobus monkey, hippopotamus, hyena, giant forest hog, lion and leopard. The reserve is a bird-watcher's paradise with a wide variety of species, and there is excellent fishing in the River Kam. The reserve headquarters is in the Forest Rest Houses at Serti, on the main road between Bali and the Mambilla Plateau. These rest houses provide self-catering accommodation at a small fee.

The entrance to the reserve is about 15 km south of Serti. In the dry season, it is possible to drive to the former headquarters at Gashaka village, some 30 km from the entrance gate, where more self-catering accommodation is available. The reserve is best explored on foot and it is possible to hire game guards, guides and porters at either Serti or in Gashaka village. Visitors planning to climb Chappal Waddi should collect a game guard from Serti and drive up to Njawai in the north-east corner of the plateau. Porters can be hired at Njawai and a 2-day trek is then needed to reach the top of the mountain.

Gashaka-Gumti is a most valuable resource, which has recently been neglected. It urgently deserves attention as it is one of the most important conservation areas in Nigeria.
For **Route** and **Hotels** see Mambila Plateau on page 55.

Ikot-Ekpene

Ikot-Ekpene is in Akwa Ibom State. It is located on the road from Aba to Calabar but very close to Aba. It has an excellent tourist market on the left side of the road at Ikot-Ekpene junction. The variety of goods is first-class, with traditional musical instruments, handbags, wood carvings, masks and various other items of interest. Be prepared to bargain hard. A rule of thumb is to offer about a third of the price asked, and move upwards until you can reach an agreement.

Igbo-Ukwu

This is a small town, south-east of Onitsha. It was here that, by chance, in 1938, a man found some bronze artefacts while digging a well, but it was not until 1958 that the site was fully excavated by an English archaeologist, Thurstan Shaw, who revisited the site in 1989. The bronzes are dated to about the 9th century. Apart from this important discovery, the town has no other significance. Most of the bronzes are now in the National Museum in Lagos, but when the author visited the village in 1989 there was a museum being built which will house the village chief's collection of artefacts.

Makurdi

General

Makurdi is the capital of Benue State, and it is here that the main A3 road bridge crosses the Benue River, beside the railway bridge. Makurdi is a good staging post en route north or south of the Benue River. There is a good new hotel there, and another under construction. The villages near Makurdi, south of the Benue, are interesting as they have a distinctive Tiv design, with a circular, open-sided meeting structure in the centre of the village. There is the Ikwe Holiday Resort, with chalets and a conference hall, approximately 20 km to the east of Makurdi along the Katsina Ala road but turning into another road heading south. The resort is not yet fully-developed. For up-to-date information on this Holiday Resort, enquire at the Benue State Liaison Office in Victoria Island, Lagos.

Route

Since the new bridge across the Niger at Ajaokuta has been opened, the quickest route from Lagos to Makurdi is now via this bridge and thence to Ayangba, Ankpa, and the new road to Makurdi. At the time of writing, the road through Ankpa town was laterite, but all the rest of this route from the Niger is along good roads, and the journey can be done in 7 hours.

Hotels

The new *Benue Hotel* which is situated on a hill overlooking the Benue River, was opened in October 1989, and is to be recommended. The *Makurdi Plaza* is a slightly less-expensive alternative. Work on the new *Sheraton Hotel,* which was suspended, was due to begin again in 1990, and when completed it would be an excellent place to stay as it has a commanding position on a hill overlooking the Benue River.

All the 3 hotels are in the same area, and as a broad guide the hotels are all on the hill with the tall radio masts. At the main roundabout in the town, turn north and cross the railway line. Fork right off the dual carriageway where it curves to the left, and continue up the hill until you reach the Benue Hotel on the right, and the Sheraton a little further on. To get to the Makurdi Plaza, turn sharp right immediately after the right fork, and it is signed to the Hotel.

Mambilla Plateau

General

The Mambilla Plateau is in the south-east corner of Gongola State, which shares a border with the Cameroons. It is a high grassland plateau averaging over 1219 m, which is scenic, cool and a pleasant change from the heat and humidity of Lagos. Unfortunately, it is not easily accessible at present as the approach roads are some of the worst encountered in the country. It is recommended that a 4-wheel drive vehicle with good suspension is used, and that visitors take all essentials, especially petrol, plenty of drinking water and possibly, camping equipment and food. There is no good hotel on the plateau, the roads are rough - to say the least - and the main town, Gembu, has few facilities. Power cuts are frequent and there are no telephones. However, it is a very attractive and interesting area and well worth a visit if you are well-prepared, as the area has cattle ranches, tea plantations and rolling grassy hills. It is very different from the rest of Nigeria in regard to flora and fauna, and is home to some rare species of birds and animals, especially at the Gashaka Game Reserve.

It is possible (but only in a 4-wheel drive vehicle) to drive into Cameroon from Gembu, across the Donga river via a 'punted' ferry and down a steep escarpment, but this is not for the faint-hearted or a vehicle with weak brakes. The route is normally only used by smugglers and intrepid travellers and it is essential to take advice before attempting it; we drove up the escarpment from the Cameroons in a Range Rover which tested the vehicle to the very limits.

Route

The best route to Mambilla is through Lagos - Benin City - Onitsha - Enugu - Otukpo - Yandev - Katsina Ala - Wukari - Mutum Biyu - Bali - Serti - Gembu, although an alternative is to cross the

Niger by the new bridge at Ajaokuta, then go to Ankpa and thence to Otukpa and Otukpo, etc. In early 1990, the road from Enugu to Katsina Ala via Abakaliki had a very bad stretch and it was best to take the longer route via Otukpo and Yandev to Katsina Ala. The road via Takum and South Gida was also very bad in early 1989. So, again, it is advisable to take the alternative route via Wukari. Do not be tempted to take the short-cut from Yandev to Mbatie and Zaki Biam. As at 1989 there was no ferry over the Katsina Ala River. The road between Bali and Jamtari was badly damaged but from near Jamtari to the foot of the escarpment, however, there is an excellent new road. The road up the escarpment onto the plateau from Mayo Selbe was completed in 1990. It is better to travel in the dry season than in the slippery mud of the wet season. It is a 3-day journey from Lagos to Gembu. From Bali, it will take at least 6 hours hard driving and it would be very unwise to drive in the dark. There is an alternative route onto the plateau via Baissa, but part of this was washed away in March 1989 and it may take a long time to repair, so do not attempt this route without checking first.

Hotels

There is a basic *Government Guest House* in Gembu which can be booked through the Gongola State Liaison Office in Lagos, and a simple hotel called *The Daula*. It is also possible, with permission, to stay at the tea plantation owned by the Nigerian Beverage Production Company. They have no office in Lagos, but their headquarters is at Yola, next to the airport, and a request for accommodation could be sent to them by courier service, but this is a privilege, not a right. The Upper Benue River Basin Authority also have a Guest House, near the Gembu airstrip, in the old forestry Department Guest House. Again, permission must be obtained first. Permission and directions can be obtained from the Department of Wildlife & Forestry in Serti.

Nsukka

Nsukka is in the north of Anambra State, due north of Enugu. Its claim to fame is that it hosts the University of Nigeria, which is the oldest indigenous university, all the older ones having been set up before independence and affiliated with universities in England. Within the campus of the university is an excellent museum which contains stone-age relics, old pottery, traditional masks and many other interesting items connected with the area. If you are passing, or staying at Enugu, this museum is well worth a visit. It is well-laid out, has many fascinating exhibits and is not too large. Just north of the turning to Nsukka is a village with a lorry park, called Obollo-Afor. Here you can buy brightly coloured baskets (from the roadside stalls) of a type not seen elsewhere in Nigeria.

Obudu Cattle Ranch

General

The Obudu Cattle Ranch is a popular tourist site in the northeast corner of Cross River State, close to the Cameroonian border. The Obudu Plateau is over 1,524 m and the climate is cool and very pleasant. The landscape is spectacular with rolling grassland, deep-wooded valleys and waterfalls. It is best to visit Obudu in the dry season; in the rainy season much of the ranch may be covered in mist and low cloud and there are spectacular thunder storms. Sometimes between December and February the harmattan is heavy. So the best times are the end of October to December and March and April.

Tourist sites

The major attractions of the Obudu Cattle Ranch are:
a. The *waterfall* - approximately 3 hours hard walking each way. In spite of the altitude it can get very hot in the daytime

so carry plenty of water, as the walk is mostly along the tops of the grass-covered ridges. It is best to take a guide, who will lead you to the top of the waterfall where there is a shady place for a picnic. The best view of the waterfall is from across the valley, not far from the ranch.

b. *Natural swimming pool* or 'grotto'. This is only a short walk from the Ranch house and is in a pleasant shady setting. It is large enough for a quick dip but no more.

c. The *Gorilla Camp* is approximately 13 km from the hotel. So, it is a very long day's trek, (approximately 8 hours for the round trip). In 1988, it was proved that there were gorillas on the Obudu Plateau, but it is doubtful whether visitors would be lucky enough to see them, as they are very shy animals.

d. Horse riding is ₦10 per hour, and there are only a limited number of saddles.

e. Bird watching - there are many unusual species of birds at Obudu, owing to its montane habitat; so take your binoculars and field guide.

f. Sports facilities - tennis court, squash court, crazy-golf course (putting only).

g. Walking - there are many interesting walks, so take good walking shoes, and a small backpack for water, etc., and it is probably best to engage a guide. One of the best walks is along the track from the farm to the cataract, near the border with Cameroon.

It is wise to book the chalets beforehand as the hotel can be full at peak times like public holidays and weekends, and it can be done in one of the following ways:

a. Through the Cross River State Liaison Office, Victoria Island, Lagos (near Bar Beach).
b. Write to the Obudu Cattle Ranching Co. Ltd., P O Box 37, Obudu, Cross River State.
c. Radio through to the Ranch from the Obudu Local Government office, in Obudu town.
d. Obudu Cattle Ranch Office, No 2 Barracks Road, ADC Building, Calabar,

Route

The direct route is through Lagos - Benin City - Enugu - Abakaliki - Ogoja; turn right to Vandeikya and Obudu town (the turning is unsigned). However, the Abakaliki road was in very bad condition as at the time of writing and we were advised to go via Otukpa - Otukpo - Yandev - Katsina Ala and then turn left off the Ogoja road towards Vandeikya. It was a longer route, as our informant said, it had taken him 3 or 4 hours to travel 100 km on the Abakaliki route; and obviously the wiser choice. If it is possible, take up-to-date advice on the state of these roads. In Obudu turn left at a T-junction near the Post Office and follow the road towards Ikom. Approximately 4 km from Obudu, the cattle ranch is signed to the left, and from there it is approximately another 60 km to the ranch. Once you reach the ranch entrance at the bottom of the plateau you begin to climb very steeply for the last 11 km. There are 20 hairpin bends so make sure your brakes are in good condition! The road surface is good but, of course, the gradient is very steep. It is at least a 12-hour journey from Lagos, and it is better to break the journey at Enugu where the recommended hotel is the Nike Lake Hotel (see section on Enugu, page 51). If you are visiting Calabar, the route is via Ikom, and will take you up to 5 hours.

Hotels

The ranch has a hotel with chalets. The accommodation consists of:

a. 11 VIP chalets (4 rooms in each)
b. 6 suites
c. 16 single rooms

The hotel has a dining room which is not expensive and serves basic food, normally with a set menu and no choice. It is advisable to take some of your own food for picnics, etc.

Ogbunike Cave

This cave is just south of the Onitsha-Enugu expressway, a few kilometres from Onitsha. It has not been developed as a tourist site, as it is a shrine for the local people, so you must gain permission from a guide at St Monica's Secondary School nearby before entering it, and then negotiate a good price for the guide's services. The cave is in a small valley and there is a large entrance to the first cave, but it is possible to crawl through a tunnel for a hundred metres or so, and emerge further down the valley. There are small bats roosting in one of the tunnels and strange spiders and insects can be seen by shining a torch onto the roof of the main cave. Children who like 'spooky' experiences would enjoy this cave, but wear old clothes and take a torch. It is essential to take a guide.

Route

The cave is near the village of Ogbunike on the Onitsha - Awka (pronounced Oka) road, From the direction of Onitsha, when you reach Ogbunike look for a sign on the left of the road printed 'St Monica's Secondary School'. Follow this road (potholed) for about 2 km until you reach the school. Ask for a guide, who will then unlock the barrier and you can drive another kilometre on a dirt track to the parking place above the cave.

Oguta Lake Resort

General

The Oguta Lake Resort has a motel near the lake, an 18-hole golf course, a tennis court and table-tennis. There is also a children's playground and an old Civil War bunker, (the 'Ojukwu Bunker'), which is close to the Club House on the golf course. The motel is set in peaceful surroundings with pleasant walks, and the staff are friendly and helpful.

The motel has rooms for about 60 made up of presidential suites and double rooms. The golf course is not up to European championship standards but is satisfactory. The village of Oguta on the other side of the lake can be reached by car-ferry or canoe, and it is possible to hire a motor boat for excursions. If you are in the area, Oguta is worth a visit as an alternative to staying at Owerri. Regattas are sometimes held on the lake.

Route

The Oguta Lake Resort is north-west of Owerri, the capital of Imo State and the town of Oguta is marked on most road maps. The route is Lagos - Benin City - Onitsha - turn south towards Owerri - turn right (west) at Mgbidi and when you get to Oguta town, ask for directions to the car-ferry. The ferry runs every 20 minutes or so across the kilometre wide lake, and can take several cars. From the landing stage, it is only $\frac{1}{2}$ km to the motel. If you are approaching from Owerri there is no need to take a ferry. Turn left off the main Owerri - Onitsha road at Ogbaku, and continue along the road until you reach a T-junction. Turn right and you will soon reach the motel opposite the golf course.

Onitsha

Onitsha is on one of the major bridge crossings over the River Niger, in Anambra State. It has always been an important commercial city, showing great enterprise and entrepreneurial skills. The main market in Onitsha is said to be the largest and best-stocked in West Africa. To see it all takes the best part of a day. Most travellers pass through Onitsha on their way to Enugu and places east. Onitsha has no modern hotels and the only hotel that has been mentioned by a fellow traveller is the *Heritage,* on Heritage Drive, which is said to be satisfactory. Some of the roads in the town are badly affected by water erosion, which can seriously delay traffic.

Oron

Oron is in the south-east corner of Akwa-Ibom State, on the Cross River, and is worth visiting for its National Museum. The museum, which overlooks the river, is next to the embarkation point for the Calabar car-ferry. The museum is mainly about the local Ibibio tribe and has an important collection of wooden Ekpu memorial carvings, which portray the male ancestors of the Ibibio people. They are believed to be between 2 and 3 centuries old. The importance of the Oron carvings was first recognised when Kenneth C Murray, then an Art master at the Teacher's Training College, Uyo, observed them in 1938. Unfortunately, many of the Ekpu carvings were destroyed in the civil war, but there is still a significant number left. Near the museum kitchen there is a well-preserved civil war bunker, as this was an important defensive point overlooking the river.

The ferry to Calabar goes once a day and takes 2 hours, but does not run at very regular times. Oron is about an hour's drive from Uyo, the state capital, but shortly before reaching the town there were several kilometres of laterite road as at 1990. There is the *Metropolitan Hotel* in Uyo near the State House, which is adequate. There are plans to build a new hotel in Uyo soon.

Owerri

Owerri is the capital of Imo State. Imo is mostly a one-ethnic group state inhabited by the Igbo people. The Igbos are renowned for their music and dancing, especially their masquerades when the dancers wear elaborate masks. Owerri itself is dominated by the Assumpta Catholic Cathedral which towers

Don't say Gin – say GILBEY'S

Distilled and bottled by
International Distillers Nigeria Limited, Otta.
Lagos Office: 15 Commercial Avenue, Yaba. Tel: 865447

above all other buildings in the centre of the town and is one of the cleanest and best laid-out cities in Nigeria. The only places of interest to visit are the Mbari Cultural Centre and Museum, and the Zoological Garden, Nekede, on the outskirts of the town.

Route
Lagos - Benin City - Onitsha - Owerri.

Hotels
The *Imo Concorde Hotel* is one of the more modern hotels in the country, with a large swimming pool, and is definitely to be recommended. Alternatively, you can stay at the *Oguta Lake Motel,* (see page 61), which is within an hour of Owerri.

Port Harcourt

General

Port Harcourt is the capital of Rivers State and is the centre of the oil industry in Nigeria. It is called 'The Garden City' as it has many more trees and parks than most cities in Nigeria. Port Harcourt is now the second most important port in Nigeria although it did not exist before 1913. Nearby are the 2 historical ports of Bonny and Brass, which were formerly connected with the slave trade, but are now better known as oil ports and terminals.

Tourist sites

a. *The Rivers State Museum.* The museum is presently housed in the Secretariat buildings, although there are plans to move it to a specially-designed building. The museum has many examples of local culture, especially masks and carvings, and it is worth a visit.

b. *Rivers State Cultural Centre.* The State Cultural Centre is in Bonny Street which is down in the old part of the town, and has a stage and auditorium for plays and dancing and a shop where you can purchase local handicrafts.

c. *Boat trips.* Port Harcourt is at the head of the delta area and it is possible to take a boat trip down the creeks of the delta to Bonny. You will pass through mangrove swamps and see the many fishing villages along the shores of the creeks. If you go ashore at Bonny be sure to take an identitiy card as the immigration department may require proof of identity. Also, it is advisable not to photograph any of the oil installations. Bonny has an exciting festival with war canoes on Christmas Day and Opobo has a similar festival on New Year's Day.

d. *Golf Course.* There is a very pleasant and well-groomed golf course at Port Harcourt. It has recently been increased to 18 holes, and is one of the best courses in Nigeria.

f. *Azumini Blue River.* This is an attractive picnic place about an hour's drive from Port Harcourt between Akwete and Azumini. The river has beautiful clear blue water with sandy beaches. It is possible to hire a canoe to take you for a short journey along the river to one of the clean, sandy beaches where there are wooden chairs, tables and a BBQ grill provided for picnics. From Port Harcourt take the Enugu expressway for about 45 km until you reach a turning to the right between a Texaco and an AP petrol station. Continue through the village of Akwete (see page 46), until you reach the bridge over the river near Azumini. You can hire canoes from near the bridge to take you to the beaches.

Route

To get to Port Harcourt, the following route is suggested:
Lagos - Benin City - Sapele - Warri roundabout - Patani - Ahoada- Port Harcourt. The road between the turn-off to Warri and the

bridge at Patani was repaired in early 1990 and is now a good road. This route takes between 6 and 7 hours.

Hotels

The *Presidential Hotel* is the main hotel in Port Harcourt with a large swimming pool and two good restaurants; a Lebanese restaurant called the *Why Not* and a Chinese Restaurant, both serving excellent food. It receives satellite TV from Europe and America and is considered a good hotel. It can be seen on the right as you are entering Port Harcourt on the dual carriageway. Take the slip road right, shortly before the hotel. Tel: (084) 300260-2 Telex: 61308. P M B 5141.

There is another hotel called the *Olympia*, 45 Force Road, near the golf course which is in the main residential area. The location is pleasant but the service is slow.

There is also the *Airport Hotel* at the International Airport which is about 30 minutes drive from the city. It is a good alternative to the hotels in the city, especially if you are travelling by air. Tel: (084) 310400-13 and 334721.

Rojenny Tourist Village

This tourist village, which is just outside Onitsha at the kilometre 11 mark on the Onitsha - Owerri road, was still under construction as at late 1989. Once completed it should have accommodation, a restaurant, a miniature zoo, tennis courts, swimming pool, dance hall, amusement park, joy-rides and various other attractions, including a make-believe 'shrine'. The tourist village is the brain-child of Chief RA Ezeonwuka and was started in November 1986.

Umuahia National War Museum

The National War Museum is located at Ebite Amafor Isingwu on the outskirts of Umuahia, which is due east of Owerri, capital of

Imo State and close to the Enugu - Port Harcourt expressway. The museum is extremely well-laid out, very interesting and informative and a 'must' if you are in the area of Owerri or Port-Harcourt. Apart from exhibitions of war relics from pre-colonial times, there are displays of the Enugu coal miners' riot, the Aba women's riot, Tiv riots, Niger Delta and Maitatsine (Kano) religious disturbances. There is an excellent section with photographs, maps and exhibits of the Nigerian Civil War. The radio room used by the Biafrans during the war is on display, as well as tanks, aircraft, boats and weapons.

Yola

General

Yola is the capital of Gongola State, on the upper reaches of the Benue River and is close to some of the most scenic areas of Nigeria which lie along the mountainous border with Cameroon. Yola has no tourist sites itself, but it does have a fishing festival in April and is a base for touring in the area. The very scenic Mandara mountains north of Yola, (pictured in Peter Ho'mes's book, *Nigeria, Giant of Africa*) are described on page 107 of this book, but are well within reach of Yola. The Mambilla Plateau Plateau described on page 55 is within a day's journey from Yola as are the Shebshi mountains to the south.

Route

From Lagos there are several routes to Yola. One is via Benin ity - Onitsha - Enugu - Otukpo - Yandev - Katsina Ala - Wukari- Jalingo - Numan - Yola, or cross the Niger via the new bridge at Ajaokuta, and from there to Ankpa, south to Otukpa and thence to Otukpo, etc. The road from Enugu via Abakaliki was very rough in early 1990, so do not go this way without taking up-to-date advice. The road between Wukari and Numan was badly potholed in places in 1990. So, unless the road has been improved, allow extra time for your journey. There is an alternative route after Jalingo via Zing and Mayo Belwa, but the answer is to seek advice from the local taxi drivers as to the state of these roads. From Abuja, the route is through Jos - Bauchi - Gombe - Numan - Yola.

Hotels

A new luxury hotel called the *International Hotel* was opened in early 1990, and is the recommended hotel in Yola. But there are several less expensive hotels including the *Taraba Hotel* on Secretariat Road, the *Peacock Hotel* on Mubi Road and the *Hamco* on Airport Road which are all adequate for an overnight stop. The International is on Kashim Ibrahim road, Tel: (075) 25739 or 25459.

4

North-West

Introduction

General

North-west Nigeria covers the area bordered by the River Niger to the south and west, the Niger Republic to the north, and the state boundaries of Kano, Kaduna, and Abuja, the Federal Capital Terrritory, to the east. Thus, the area includes the states of Niger, Sokoto, Katsina, Kano, Kaduna and the F C T.

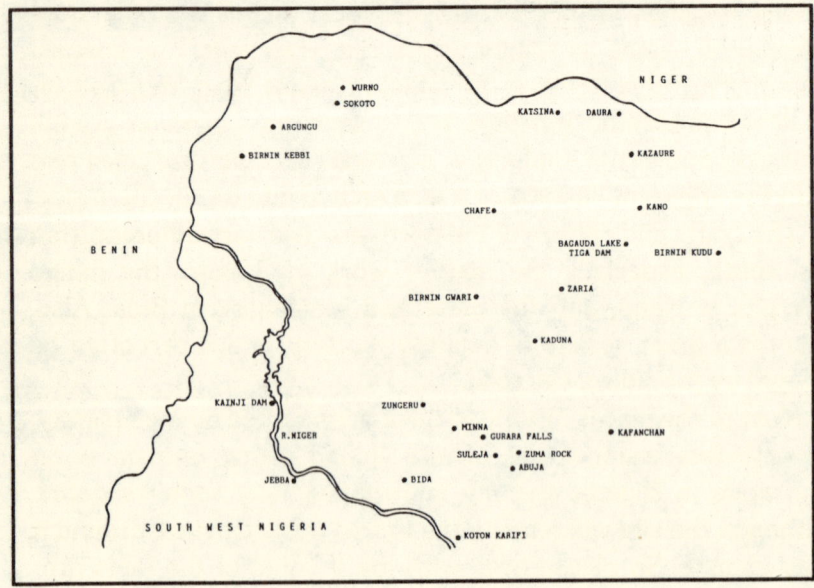

This region does not have as many tourist sites as the south of the country. But it is a very interesting area to visit, with an entirely different historical background, as traditionally it has looked north across the Sahara for its trade, rather than south to the sea. The vegetation, climate, terrain and people are also markedly different from those in the south. For this reason alone a visit to the north is a 'must' for those living in Lagos or in any of the other cities of the south.

North-west Nigeria is fascinating for its strong Hausa/Fulani traditions, walled cities, and great Sallah festivals, with its spectacular durbars. *Id el Fitri* marks the end of the Muslim period of Ramadan; *Id el Kabir* is a Muslim thanksgiving ceremony commemorating the substitution of Isaac with the sacrificial ram, and *Id el Maulud* marks the Prophet Muhammed's birthday. The internationally renowned Argungu Fishing Festival is another colourful event which is one of the great festivals of Nigeria. The landscape, which borders on the desert to the north, is studded with extraordinary inselbergs rising out of the surrounding countryside like great stone altars. In fact, many of these have strong religious significance to the local people and therefore permission should be sought before climbing them. The most astounding is Zuma Rock on the Lokoja-Kaduna road, shortly after passing the turn-off to Abuja. It is a huge mass of sheer granite towering above the landscape, streaked with vertical lines and with the apparent likeness of a face etched into its southern side.

The crafts and culture of the north are also very different from the south, especially the leather work in Sokoto, the indigo dye-pits in Kano, and the glass and metalwork in Bida. Also, there is a great variety of beautiful pottery, which can often be bought by the side of the road.

Most of the places described have been visited by me recently, nevertheless changes are always taking place; tourism is on the move in Nigeria and my information may soon be dated. Although the site will remain, the tourist infrastructure around it may change. So please bear with me if some of the facts are not up to date.

Abuja

General

Abuja needs little introduction. It is being developed as the new capital of Nigeria in 4 phases which will probably extend well into the next century. The first phase will see the main government buildings constructed, including government secretariats, the presidential palace and guest houses, libraries, museums, parks, parade grounds, local government buildings, diplomatic missions and their accompanying residences. The infrastructure for all this building is being set in place at present, with new roads, powerlines, water, sewage systems and telephone lines being constructed. Three hotels have already been completed: the excellent *Nicon-Noga Hilton* managed by the British Hilton Hotels, (part of Ladbrokes of the United Kingdom), the *Sheraton Hotel*, which opened in early 1990 and the *Agura*. A fourth hotel is planned. One of the outstanding features of this new city is the large golden domed mosque which dominates the town. It was completed in 1990.

Tourist sites

a. The plant nursery and reservoir below the Abuja inselberg.

b. Usuma dam and reservoir off the northern dual carriageway, about 40 minutes from Abuja. Consult the hotel management about gaining permission to enter the dam. A pleasant picnic spot.

c. Zuma Rock - see page 93.

d. The golf course which is being built near the Hilton Hotel and was due to be opened in late 1990.

e. Pottery market on the Lokoja-Kaduna road just before the first Abuja turn-off if you are coming from the south. A large selection of Gwari pots, jugs and bowls are on sale here. They are not expensive and are beautifully designed.

f. Gurara Falls on the Minna road - see page 79.

g. Dr Ladi Kwali's pottery at Suleja - see page 91.

Route

There are several ways of travelling to Abuja by road from Lagos. The best route is Lagos - Benin expressway - Ore - Ondo- Akure - Owo - Ipele - Kabba - Lokoja - Abuja. Alternatively, you can go via Benin City and Auchi, or via Ibadan - Jebba - Bida and Abuja. It takes between 8 and 10 hours depending on your route.

Hotels

The *Nicon-Noga Hilton* is of international standard and is one of the very best in Nigeria. It is expensive, but there are special 'Royal Weekends' with reduced rates. It has every facility including a large swimming pool, tennis courts, squash courts, gymnasium, sauna and night club. Tel: (09) 5231811 - 830. Telex 71504 HILTON NG.

The *Sheraton Hotel* also provides all the facilities of an international hotel and opened in early 1990. Tel: (09) 234225.

The smaller *Golden Tulip Agura Hotel* is on Festival Road. It has a swimming pool, tennis courts and a night club, and is a comfortable hotel. Tel: (09) 2341753 - 760. Telex: 71496 AGURA NG.

Argungu

General

Argungu is famous for its fishing festival normally held on a Saturday near the end of February/early March, but the date very much depends upon when the state government and the Emir of Argungu decide to hold it. Enquiries can be made from the Sokoto State Liaison Office, 17 Adeola Odeku St, Victoria Island, Lagos. The festival lasts for 4 days, the climax being the fishing competition, but many other activities take place during the period: archery, cultural dancing, camel and donkey racing, bicycle racing, wrestling, boxing (Nigerian style) an agricultural show, handicraft exhibition and the Kabanci display (water events). The main reason for tourists to go to Argungu is to see the fishing festival. Its origins are said to date back to the 16th century when the great Mohammed Kanta, founder of the Kebbi empire, held a festival to mark the end of the fishing season. The modern form dates back to 1934. The festival takes place at a site called the Matan Fada where a large pavilion has been built on the side of the Rima River.

Procedure for the fishing festival

Thousands of fishermen, each carrying a large gourd and 2 hand nets resembling the wings of a huge butterfly, form up in line about 500 m from the river. On a signal from the Emir, a gun is fired and the fishermen race towards the river in a sensational, mile-long charge. They pour into the river in front of the stands until it becomes a seething mass of bodies, nets and gourds, creating a magnificent sight. Judges, officials and musicians in boats steer their way in amongst the crowds of fishermen, adding to the colourful scene. The fishermen who catch the largest fish are escorted to the centre of the pavilion where their catch is weighed and both the fish and fisherman are tagged for future reference. About 2 hours after the start another gun signals the end of the contest. Then the fish are graded according to weight and a substantial price is given to the man who has caught the largest fish, with smaller prizes for the runners-up. The winning fish is normally between 30 and 50 kg. Fishing is then forbidden in this part of the river until the festival in the following year.

It pays to get to the stands early, at about 8.00 am, to get a seat. The Governor and the official party arrive around 9.30 am and the fishing competition begins at 10.00 am. It is all over by about 1.00 pm.

In summary, this festival is well worth a visit even if you can only spare the time for the final day. There is also a small museum in Argungu, in the old palace of the Emir, built in 1849, called the Kanta Museum, which is of interest as it gives an insight into the local history, culture and weaponry, including an example of the horse-armour once used in local battles, and a suit of chain mail. It has objects which are up to 500 years old, including those which belonged to Mohammed Kanta, 1516-1554, the founder of the Kebbi Empire. The villages around Argungu are also of special interest as they have attractive round granaries. In March, near the end of the dry season, the area is very arid, and camels are a familiar sight.

Route

The best route to Argungu is Lagos - Ibadan - Ilorin (or the Ilorin by-pass) - Jebba - Kontagora - Yelwa - Jega - then take the Sokoto road until the turn-off to Argungu about 20 km past Shagari, although there is an alternative, but untried, route from Jega through Kalgo and Birnin Kebbi. It is a good two-day journey by car, and after Ilorin the route is not blessed with good hotels. An alternative is to go via Abuja, but it is 2 days hard driving. Flying to Sokoto is another option, but of course, the planes will be heavily booked at the time of the festival.

Hotels

Booking for the fishing festival and reservations at the new *Grand Fishing Hotel* must be made at least one month beforehand, through the Sokoto State Liaison Office, 17 Adeola Odeku St, Victoria Island, Lagos. On arrival in Argungu, the Fishing Hotel is very obvious as it is on the left as you enter the town. If you cannot book accommodation there, try Sokoto which is about one hour's drive away on a reasonable road - see page 89 on Sokoto, for hotels.

Bagauda Lake Hotel, Tiga Dam

General

The *Bagauda Lake Hotel* has been developed as a conference centre with chalets, a swimming pool and nightclub, and is some 56 km south of Kano. Further along the road is the *Rock Castle Hotel*, overlooking the Tiga Dam and reservoir. It is in an attractive environment, but unfortunately, the hotel is under-used. It is a pleasant spot for anyone wanting to get away from the rush and bustle of Kano, but is really too far from the city for a convenient over-night stop. Tiga Dam is a pleasant picnic spot not too far from Kano.

Route

From Kano take the Zaria road towards the south, and after about 50 km there is a major turning on the left which is marked 'Bagauda Lake Hotel', although this sign may have been removed during the recent construction of the new dual carriageway. If you are uncertain, ask one of the local people to direct you. The hotel is reached after a few kilometres. The Tiga Dam and Rock Castle Hotel are approximately 24 km further down this road.

Bida

General

Bida is a fascinating town, renowned for its handicrafts, its colourful market and the fact that it is the main city of the Nupe tribe. The Emir or Etsu Nupe, has a palace in the town. Bida is famous for its glass beads, cloth, silver and brasswork, its carved 8-legged stools made from a single piece of wood, and for its decorative pottery, although the latter is only found in villages

The market, which is in the centre of the old town, soon to be modernised, is one of the most colourful traditional markets in Nigeria. The silver and brasswork may be seen on either side of the main road leading from the first town gate, (if you are coming from the west), towards the market. The beadmakers and some brassworkers are in Musaga Road, which is on the right, off the Bida by pass when you are heading towards Lapai. The turn-off is almost opposite the Lafiya Clinic which you can see on the left of the road. The beadmakers, whose raw materials are melted beer bottles and coloured glass jars, are about 400 m on the left and the brassworkers a little further up the road, on the right. If you agree to offer them some 'dash', the craftsmen will allow you to watch them make their beads and bangles, using an earthenware kiln and handmade bellows. Some interesting pottery can be bought near the Kaduna River bridge on the Bida side. Nearby villages have similar pottery for sale as well as the 8-legged Bida stools.

Route
From Lagos you go through Ibadan - Ilorin (or Ilorin by-pass) - Jebba, - turn right just after Mokwa - Bida. You arrive on the Bida bypass which skirts the north of the town. The old town is to your right through the gates, but see directions above to the beadmakers. The journey takes between 7 and 8 hours from Lagos.

From Abuja, take the northern dual-carriageway out of the city onto the Kaduna road. Turn left towards Suleja and Minna shortly after passing Zuma Rock. Turn left (south-west) at Lambatta, through Lapai to Bida.

Hotels
Unfortunately, there are no good hotels in Bida, though there is a Catering Rest House in the Government Residential Area. An alternative is to make it a day's outing from Abuja or Minna. See pages 70 and 89 for hotels in these towns.

Birnin Gwari

General

Birnin Gwari is a wildlife reserve. Although it has none of the larger game animals, it has monkeys, baboons, warthog, etc. It is also excellent for bird-watching. You may see the rare ground hornbill, which is almost the size of a turkey, in the area. The reserve is not as well-known or as well-preserved as the main reserves in Nigeria, but could make an interesting stop, although there is only basic accommodation. If you are in the area, the Dogon Rafi river is also worth a visit, especially for bird-watchers. The end of the dry season is the best time to visit. Please note that there are *two* Birnin Gwari in Kaduna State shown on the map, but the Game Reserve is the one near the village due west of Kaduna: the southern Birnin Gwari.

Route

Kaduna is the best base for visiting the reserve. Take the Lagos road from Kaduna to Birnin Gwari, and after the village there is a turning to the left. The Wildlife Officer's bungalow is down this road on the left. The reserve itself is approximately 1 km further down the Lagos road, but to the right of the road. The chalets overlooking the lake, beside the main road in Birnin Gwari, provide very basic accommodation, but there is no restaurant.

To get to the Dogon Rafi river, drive to Birnin Gwari from the Kaduna direction, and in the middle of the village there is a junction just after the water tower. Turn right (Funtua road) and proceed for 11 km until you reach a construction camp and quarry. The hamlet just after that is Kungi and at the end of the village is a track to the left. Follow this track for 3 km until you come to a waterfall and from there you can walk along the river.

Birnin Kebbi

Birnin Kebbi is an old traditional Hausa walled town in Sokoto State south-west of Argungu, and makes an interesting stop if you are touring the north-west, or visiting the Argungu Fishing Festival.

Birnin Kudu

Birnin Kudu is known for its rock paintings, similar to those found in the Sahara. The paintings are of cattle and wild animals, but the ones we saw were small and not very clear, and the protective cage around them rather detracted from their effect. There are paintings on both sides of the main road. Those on the left are the clearer. It is necessary to get a guide to show you the paintings when you reach Birnin Kudu, which is south-east of Kano on the A237 road to Maiduguri. There is no good hotel in the area, so it is only worth visiting if you are passing through Birnin Kudu. The nearest base for visiting this area is either Kano or Bauchi.

Chafe

Chafe is mentioned only because of its market which is held on a Sunday. It is 128 km from Zaria on the Sokoto road between Funtua and Gusau. It is a traditional Fulani market and apart from the interesting variety of livestock, both leather workers and calabash carvers can be seen at work. Fulani hats and their decorative rugs are also on sale. Also, many Fulani come to the market in their traditional dress which makes it a colourful sight. You may chance upon a Fulani bride-choosing ceremony or their manhood-proving contests when the young men beat each other with sticks, and vie to become 'the bravest of the brave'. We have witnessed both in our travels, although neither was in Chafe. The Fulani do not seem to mind being photographed; it enhances their reputation for good looks, but it is always better to ask first. Like many of the other fascinating markets in the north, it is well worth a visit if you are passing through Chafe on a Sunday.

Daura

General

Daura is a historical town owing to its position as the spiritual home of the Hausa. With Katsina, it was an important trading town, but it has since declined owing to changes in the trading patterns in the north of Nigeria. There are various legends about the origins of the Hausa kingdoms. The most popular is the legend that Bayajidda Abuyazidu, son of Abdulahi, King of Baghdad, left home after a quarrel with his father in 900 AD. He came to Daura via the Kingdom of Borno, where he married the daughter of the Mai of Borno. He was later forced to flee because the Mai was jealous of him. He took his wife and concubine, Gwari, with him.

On arriving at Daura he asked for a drink, but was informed that a snake called Sarki, which lived in the well, only allowed water to be drawn on a Friday. Bayajidda was not having this, so he went to the well to draw water. The snake rose up to strike the intruder but Bayajidda struck off the snake's head with his sword. The Queen of Daura was deeply impressed and married Bayajidda for his bravery. They had a son called Bawo, who in turn had six sons who later became the rulers of Daura, Kano, Rano, Katsina, Zaria and Gobir.

These six states, together with Biram ruled by Bayajidda's son born of the Mai's daughter, formed the 'Hausa Bokwa' or seven legitimate Hausa states. It is of further interest that the concubine, Gwari, bore Karbagari, whose seven sons founded and ruled over their own states, namely Kebbi, Yauri, Gwari, Nupe, Kwororafa (Jukun), Zamfara and Yoruba (Ilorin). These latter seven states are known as the 'Banza Bokwa' meaning the seven bastard or illegitimate Hausa states. This story is told because of its significance to the present Hausa emirates, and because it is possible to visit the well at Daura even today.

The well is in a modern concrete building, but inside it is suitably decorated, with the sword of Bayajidda and a plaque com-

Abuja Mosque at night

Gwari village near Abuja

Argungu Fishing Festival

Nupe craftsmen, Bida

Gurara Falls, between Suleja and Minna

Jacaranda Restaurant, Kaduna

Entrance to the Emir's Palace, Kano

The Emir of Katsina at the Sallah Festival, Katsina

memorating the killing of the snake. It is said that if you drink from the well, you will always return to Daura. The town is a traditional Hausa 'desert' town and the gate, through which Bayajidda is said to have entered, is still standing. Daura holds a Sallah celebration at all 3 muslim festivals, *Id-el-Fitri, Id-el-Kabir* and *Id-el-Maulud,* although the Durbar is smaller than the one at Katsina. Daura is due north of Kano and due east of Katsina. There is no suitable hotel there, so it is best to stay in Kano.

Route

From Kano, there is a good tarred road due north to Daura.

Gurara Falls

General

Gurara Falls are on the Gurara River in Niger State, on the road between Suleja and Minna. The falls are very impressive in the wet season, but by the end of the dry season they are greatly reduced. They are approximately 200m wide with a drop of about 30m and in the rains they have a large amount of water cascading over the top, creating rainbows in the spray below. You can climb down a steep path to the water's edge beneath the falls, although there is a good viewing spot and covered picnic place where you can take photographs without having to do the climb! There is a plan to develop Gurara into a conference centre, with a marina, and golf course, but unfortunately this would ruin the charm of this natural, peaceful site. Gurara Falls is well worth a visit for a picnic lunch or even as a camping site, but it is necessary to bring all your own requirements, as the small bar is not always open. The nearest hotels are at Abuja or Minna.

Route

From Abuja, take the northern dual carriageway to the main Kaduna road. Turn right and shortly after passing Zuma Rock, turn left at a major turning towards Suleja. From Suleja take the Minna road for approximately 32 km, then shortly after going past the turning to Bida at Lambatta, (about 4 km) you will see a sign on the right saying 'Nigeria's No. 1 Tourist Attraction'. Go down this road for another 4 km and you will come to the top of the falls.

Kaduna
General

Kaduna used to be the colonial capital of Northern Nigeria. It is on the Kaduna River. It has an airport and a railway station and is an important junction with roads branching off in 5 different directions. It is a major communications centre and industrial base in the north, and a thriving modern town. For the tourist, it is an excellent base from which to explore the surrounding countryside, with its many interesting inselbergs and pleasant spots to visit. Anyone living near, or visiting Kaduna for any length of time should try and obtain the British Advisory Team Travel Notes, which were originally started by the author in Kaduna in 1979, but subsequently up-dated by others. These are very helpful and give much greater local detail than is possible in this guide. Within Kaduna, there is little of tourist interest apart from the museum, the market and the River Gardens which are a pleasant place to walk. The iron footbridge, built in 1880, was moved from Zungeru, Lord Lugard's former capital, to its present site in the gardens in 1920, when Kaduna became the new capital of Northern Region.

There is a small National Museum on Ali-Akilu Road with wood carvings, masks and a few examples of Nok terracotta figures and Benin bronzes. There is a craft area with a craft shop behind the museum where you can watch the craftsmen at work. It is open daily from 9.00 am to 6.00 pm. There are 2 other places with small displays of traditional clothing, etc.: one at the Ministry of Information, Hospital Road, and another at the Secretariat, Sardauna Hall.

There is a polo tournament held in Kaduna in October every year and an annual trade fair between January and February. The golf course, in Golf Course Road, is an 18-hole championship course.

One 'must' for Kaduna is a visit to the *Jacaranda Restaurant and Pottery*, which is about 15 to 20 minutes drive south-east from Kaduna, out on the Kachia road. The restaurant is well-managed, has excellent food and drink and is in beautiful garden surroundings, with waterfalls, Japanese style bridges, crocodile ponds and a golf-driving range. The pottery sells first-class pottery designed along similar lines to the Suleja pottery, using natural glazes. There is also a well-run plant nursery, with the plants labelled. The restaurant is open daily for lunch. On Friday and Saturday nights, it is open for dinner. Sunday lunch is always a very popular occasion. You will not regret a visit to this restaurant, which is undoubtedly one of the best in Nigeria. There is a proposal to build chalets at the restaurant sometime in the future.

Route

There are 3 alternative routes from Lagos: the shortest is via Ibadan - Ilorin bypass - Jebba - Mokwa - Tegina, and Birnin Gwari - Kaduna. Note that the road, shown on some maps as a dotted line, north of Mokwa to Tegina (cutting off Kontagora) is now complete and a very good road. However, the stretch of road from Ibadan to (just short of) Ilorin has many bends and heavy traffic, although there are plans to make it a dual-carriageway sometime in the future. The Ilorin bypass is some 40 km north of Ogbomosho, where there is a junction signed to the left, marked 'Jebba', and this is a good straight road. The journey can be done in about 9 hours. The alternative routes are either via Benin City, Okene and Koton-Karifi or via Ore, Owo, Ipele and north to Kabba along another new road, thence to Koton-Karifi and north along the A2, but this is longer and it is advisable to break your journey overnight en route.

Hotels

Kaduna has 2 modern hotels, the *Durbar* and *Hamdala,* which are good. Both are near the Polo Ground to the north of the town, east of the main dual carriageway. The Durbar is on Independence Way, Tel: (062) 201100-8. The Hamdala, which was refurbished in 1989, is on Waff Road, Tel: (062)211005.

Outside the Hamdala are traders' stalls which sell tourist items, e.g. wood carvings, beads, Fulani blankets, baskets, etc. These are well worth a visit, but be prepared to bargain hard before you purchase.

Kafanchan/Kagoro

Kafanchan and the smaller village of Kagoro are just below the Jos escarpment on the eastern border of Kaduna State. It is a very scenic spot bordered by steep hills. From Kaduna, it is on the southern route to Jos, via Kachia. From Abuja, take the road east to Keffi, and then turn north towards Kachia. Turn right (east), at Kwoi and continue until you reach Kafanchan.

Tourist sites

a. *The waterfall.* The fall is over a 'cliff' about 30 m high with a deep pool at the base, and is naturally more impressive in the wet season. It is necessary to walk down the river, along the bank to reach the sandy beach by the falls where there is a pleasant picnic spot. From Kagoro, take the road towards Kafanchan until you come to a roundabout. Turn right along a tarmac road which later becomes laterite. Continue roughly parallel to the railway line, but when in doubt keep right until you reach the top of the falls.

b. *Railway engine graveyard.* Kafanchan is a railway junction: one line going from Jos to Kaduna and the other going south. Near the railway station are workshops and sidings, and in the sidings are about 10 old steam locomotives. They are rapidly deteriorating, but nevertheless for railway-buffs or small boys this place is well worth a visit. From Kagoro, take the road to Kafanchan, turn left at the roundabout, go past the station, follow the road over the railway, bear left and then follow the road to the right. The old engines can be seen quite clearly. The author last visited this place in 1989 and there were still some good examples of River Class steam-engines, and Canadian diesel locomotives. However, it is important to get permission from the engineer in charge, before entering the engines.

c. *Kagoro Boy Scout Camp.* Some years ago, a Boy Scout Jamboree was held at Kagoro, and some of the camp still remains. Although the huts are now derelict, it makes a good base for camping, (which we did in 1980), as there is shade and a clean stream for washing. Unfortunately, when we visited it again in 1989, it was very overgrown. It would still be possible to camp if you were prepared to clear the site a little first, as it is a good starting point for walks up the escarpment, and is close to the Kagoro Forest, an excellent place for bird-watching. If you are coming from Kaduna, drive through Kagoro in the direction of Jemma and Jos, and 200 m after the railway crossing at the end of the town, turn left onto a track beside a cactus hedge. Follow the track, cross a wooden bridge and turn right after 700 m by a large tree. Turn left about 300 m further on opposite some houses on the right. Cross another wooden bridge, and you will reach the old Scout Camp; a few minutes with a machete should provide you with a campsite!

d. The *Kagoro Forest,* a few kilometres down the road towards Jemma and Jos, is a unique area of rainforest of a type not normally found in northern Nigeria, with species of flora and fauna usually seen much further south. This forest is of special interest to bird-watchers and botanists.

Hotels

Kafanchan has a *Catering Resthouse,* and there is a small hotel in Kagoro, but I have not personally tried it out; so my advice is to camp there in the dry season or to make it a day trip from Jos, about $1\frac{1}{2}$ to 2 hours away.

Kano

General

Kano is the largest city in the north but there is a great contrast between the old Hausa city and the modern, industrial one with its international airport and railway station. It is a communications centre with main roads branching out on all points of the compass, joining the other main centres of population in Northern Nigeria. Historically, it has been a centre of trade, especially towards the north across the Sahara and south to Zaria. The Emir of Kano is one of the senior emirs in the north and his palace is in the old part of Kano, near the museum. Kano has much to offer the tourist and the photographer.

Tourist sites

a. *The Gidan Makama Museum.* The museum is near the Emir's palace and is excellent, as it shows the history of Kano, and the Hausa and Fulani people and some history of the rest of northern Nigeria. It is well worth a visit, not only for its contents, and for its shops selling arts and crafts, but also for the shape and construction of its very old building which is a national monument of architectural excellence. The museum was being renovated when we visited Kano in late 1989.

b. *The Dye Pits.* The dye pits are by the side of the road at Kofar Mata in Kano. The large vats filled with indigo dye are sunk into the ground, and the dyed cloth is laid out to dry beside them, and then beaten to obtain a high gloss. The full procedure for dyeing the cloth is best explained by one of the guides in the area. Do not take photographs without permission, which will probably require some 'dash'. The pits themselves are a little disappointing, and the area is far from clean, but do not be put off. Ask for a briefing on the dyeing from someone who speaks English and you will be surprised what you learn. Kano is not the only place which has dye-pits, but it is the best known.

c. *Emir's Palace.* The Emir's palace is worth a visit to see the old walls and the entrance gate. Kano is famous for its old walls around the older part of the city. It is 17.5 km in circumference and has 16 gates. One of the best places to see it is near the Central Mosque (see below). The Emir holds two Sallah festivals each year.

d. *Central Mosque.* The mosque is one of the largest in Nigeria, and is a fine looking building. With permission, you may be allowed up one of its minarets in order to have a good view of the city below. You are not allowed into the Mosque, itself, unless you are a muslim, of course.

e. *Kurmi Market.* There are at least 6 markets in the city, but the Kurmi market is in the old city. It is worth a visit for those who are not acquainted with northern city markets. The market is at the Makwarari/Dinki Quarters. It sells calabashes, beads, leatherwork, pottery, etc. It is best to have a guide, if possible.

f. *Kano Zoo.* The Kano Zoo is south of Kano on the Zaria road. It is west of Gyadi-Gyadi village at Gandom Aldasa. The 25-acre zoo is said to be worth a visit, especially for children.

Route

The quickest route to Kano from Lagos, if you do not go by air, is via Kaduna. There is a new dual-carriageway from Kano to Kaduna. This will therefore not only be faster, but safer. The The Zaria to Kaduna road had the reputation of being the most dangerous road in Nigeria, but with the new road fully operational this will no longer be the case. The journey from Lagos to Kano is a good 2-day journey as the complete distance is over 1,000 km.

Hotels

There are 2 large hotels in Kano, but neither is particularly new. The *Central Hotel* is on Bompai Road, Tel: (064) 600520,621042. Telex 77151 NG CENTEL. The *Daula Hotel* is at 150M Murtala Mohammed Way. Tel: (064) 600590. An alternative is the *Peking Chinese Restaurant* in Bompai Road, which also has a limited number of rooms for overnight visitors. Tel: (064) 625146.

Katsina

General

Katsina is one of the northernmost cities in Nigeria. It is on the edge of the Sahel area, bordering the country of Niger, with which it has had historical trading links for many centuries. Katsina is one of the old walled Hausa cities and is the capital of the recently created Katsina State. The city-walls were built by Queen Amina in the 16th century and have 7 gates. The gate through which Lord Lugard entered Katsina in 1903 is known as Kofar Yandaka, and a plaque commemorates the occasion. The Goborau Minaret is probably the most picturesque tourist attraction. It is the tallest mud-brick building in Nigeria and is said to be about 250 years old. A fine view of Katsina can be gained from the top, but please get permission to enter the minaret beforehand. The Emir of Katsina holds a most colourful and interesting Sallah during Muslim festivals of *Id-el-Fitri* (end of

DAF International

DAF International is a worldwide organisation committed to meeting current and future transport needs. There's a wider range of products than ever before, a more comprehensive distributor network and superb parts and service back-up. The DAF International product range of light vans, buses and trucks is designed to meet every conceivable transport application and is built to the highest quality standards utilising some of the world's most sophisticated design, testing and manufacturing techniques. DAF International – Total Transport Capability.

DAF International Limited,
Regents Place, Regent Road, Salford,
Manchester M5 4DT, UK.
Telephone: 061 873 2000.
Telex: 668137 DAFINT G.
Fax: 061 848 9020.

for high STANDARDS *of* SECURITY *you need* HIGH POWER PROFESSIONALISM

THE LION OF AFRICA INSURANCE CO. LTD.

THE LION OF AFRICA INSURANCE CO. LTD.
Head Office: St. Peters House, 3, Ajele Street P. O. Box 2055 Lagos
Telephone: 600950 - 5, Telefax 636111, Telex 23536 A/B Zaki Cables: Zaki Lagos
Branches: Enugu, Ibadan, Kaduna, Kano, Maiduguri, Port-Harcourt and Yola

A MEMBER OF THE NIGERIAN INSURANCE ASSOCIATION

A Member Company of the worldwide Guardian Royal Exchange Assurance Group.

Ramadan) and *Id-el-Kabir.* The respective dates of these two festivals depend upon the sighting of a new moon and are declared by the Sultan of Sokoto. The dates vary each year, but an English Letts diary can help your planning, as it marks the quarters of the moon. In the case of *Id-el-Fitri,* it is normally 30 days from the beginning of Ramadan. In 1989, the Sallahs were in early May and July, respectively, which gives a rough guide.

The Sallah at Katsina includes a procession of horsemen and camels, acrobats, jugglers, snake charmers and various other entertainers. At Katsina a spectacular charge (or 'jahi') by the chiefs and courtiers on horseback is included, as a salute to the Emir. The celebrations normally start at about 8.00 am. with the brilliantly attired horsemen arriving in the main square in front of the Emir's Palace. They then gather outside the city walls for prayers before returning at about 10.00 am. The Emir and his retinue enter the square and when all are assembled, the charge takes place, after which the Emir gives a short oration and then retires to his palace. The festival continues in the square with dancing, music and other traditional activities.

Route

The best route from Lagos is via Kaduna - Zaria - Funtua - Mulumfashi - Yashi - Katsina. It is possible to make the journey in 2 days, but it is hard driving. From Kaduna it is about $5\frac{1}{2}$ - 6 hours. At present the nearest airport is at Kano, but an airport is planned for the place.

Hotels

The *Lafiya Palace Hotel* was under construction in 1989 and is intended to be of international standard. The only alternative is the *Katsina Guest Inn* which is adequate. For the Sallah, it is probably best to drive from Kano, but it means a very early start.

Koton-Karifi

Koton-Karifi is known for its bridge across the River Niger. It is a fine example of engineering owing to its length and width. Koton-Karifi is just north of Lokoja (where the Niger and the Benue rivers meet) on the main road to Abuja from Benin City.

Kazaure

Kazaure is one of the northern emirates. It is a pleasant Hausa town with an Emir's palace, but on a smaller scale than most, and is about 1 hours's drive due north of Kano. A good view of the town can be had from the hill behind the town. The market is held on a Friday. It is only worth visiting if you are passing that way, but for bird-watchers there are some interesting wetlands nearby.

Minna

General

Minna is the capital of Niger State and is on the main railway line from Lagos to Kaduna and the north, and has a small airport. It does not have many tourist sites itself except a small museum, but there are places of interest nearby. At the railway station, there is an old railway engine on display, which has been kept in good condition to commemorate the fact that Minna was an important railway junction in the past. A potential tourist site is the large hydro-electric dam and power station at Shiroro on the Kaduna River, north-east of Minna. Take the Owada road and continue due north over the railway line to the dam, but it is necessary to get permission from NEPA first. See page 79 for directions to Gurara Falls, an hour or more from Minna in the direction of Abuja.

Minna has recently had an extensive road-building programme and there is now a direct road to Bida. In the future, it is hoped to have a good direct road to Kaduna, up the line of the Kaduna River. There has been a bypass constructed round the south of Minna.

Route

From Lagos the route is Ibadan - Ilorin (or Ilorin bypass) - Jebba - Mokwa - Bida - Minna. The road from Bida to Minna shown as a dotted line on some maps is now complete. From Bida, the turn-off to Minna is clearly marked to the left, a few kilometres outside the town, on the Lapai road. Do not take the old road via Wushishi unless you have plenty of time to spare!

Hotels

The *Shiroro Hotel* on the newly-constructed bypass is the best hotel in Minna.

Sokoto

General

Sokoto is the centre of Islamic activities in Nigeria. It is the home of the Sultan of Sokoto, the spiritual leader of muslims in the country. It is also the capital of Sokoto State. The city is well-laid out with avenues of neem trees, wide roads and large roundabouts, and seems like an oasis in a semi-desert area. The area around the river is an attractive place to walk in the evening, with fishermen bringing in their nets and herdsmen watering their herds. Sokoto is another of the great trading cities of the north, with old trade routes across the Sahara to Morocco and Algeria. It is famed for its excellent leatherwork including handbags, pouffes, wallets, fans, etc. Sokoto has an airport also. It is also one of the main starting points for the drive across the Sahara to North Africa and Europe.

The old Sokoto market was burnt down, but there is now a modern central market. It is still very colourful and has many items of interest, e.g. Fulani blankets, leatherwork, beads, rush mats and other handicrafts, many coming from Niger across the border. There is also a camel market, and camels are a frequent sight in Sokoto State. The old part of the town is full of character and you may see snake charmers at work.

Tourist sites

a. *The Sultan's Palace.* The palace is worth a visit to see the building, the guards in their multicoloured robes. At 9.00 pm on Thursdays, one could watch the musicians and praise-singers honour the Sultan. The palace is on Sultan Bello Road, to the north-east of the old town of Sokoto.

b. *Usman dan Fodio's Tomb.* Usman dan Fodio led the Fulani Jihad against Sultan Yunfa, the Hausa ruler of Gobir, in 1804. The Fulani came from Senegal and were in the minority to the Hausa at the time of the uprising. Both the town and nomadic cattle Fulani ganged together because they feared that they might be driven out by the concerned Hausa. Usman dan Fodio was conserned that the Hausa were not strict muslims and wished to see that some of their pagan ways were eliminated. The jihad was successful because the Hausa rulers were not united and by 1808 all the main rulers in Zaria, Daura, Kano, Bauchi, Gobir, Katsina, Kebbi and Zamfara had been defeated. The jihad spread to Adamawa, Nupe and Ilorin, but failed to suceed in Borno. Usman dan Fodio's tomb is, therefore, of great significance to muslims in Nigeria. It is not a tourist site as such, but of great historical importance. Women are not allowed inside the tomb, and you should ask permission if you wish to photograph the entrance. For more information read *Essentials of West African History,* Book One, by J Akin Akinyemi.

c. *Sokoto Museum.* The present Sokoto Museum is in the History Bureau not far from the Sultan's palace. In 1990, a National Museum was said to be under construction on the bypass.

d. *Clapperton's Tomb.* Clapperton, the great English explorer, who was accompanied by Richard Lander, died in Sokoto and was buried there. This will be of interest to historians. Anyone interested should ask for further information at the History Bureau.

Route

The shortest route to Sokoto by road is Lagos - Ibadan - Ilorin - (or Ilorin bypass) - Jebba - Kontagora - Yelwa - Jega - Sokoto. This is a 2-day journey. The alternative route, if you are travelling via Abuja, is Kaduna - Zaria - Funtua - Gusau - Sokoto, but of course this is much longer.

Hotels

Sokoto has a number of hotels. The most modern is the *Giginya* which was completed in 1988. It is on the ByePass, not far from the airport. Tel: (060) 231263, 231670. The other good hotel is the *Shakura Hotel* which is closer to the centre of the town, and the older *Sokoto Hotel* is next door.

Suleja

General

Suleja is famous for the *Ladi Kwali Pottery,* which used to be known as the Abuja Pottery before the town was renamed 'Suleja'. The pottery was set up with the help of Michael Cardew, and Dr Ladi Kwali, who was his renowned pupil. The pottery staff are happy to show visitors around and you can purchase pottery either in its finished glazed state or in the 'terracotta' stage. The pottery is of a high standard and the traditional designs are most interesting - one of the women potters we saw had the designs of lizards, snakes, and butterlies tattooed on her arms. It is worth a visit and should not be missed if you are visitting either Abuja or Minna.

Route

Suleja is on the Abuja - Minna road just to the west of the main road (A2) which runs from Lokoja to Kaduna. Enter Suleja along the main road from the A2, turn left (south) into the main street at the T-junction, and continue along this road, over a narrow bridge and you will see the pottery on your left shortly afterwards. It has a sign outside it, but if you are in doubt, ask; it is well-known.

Wurno

Wurno is 30 km north-east of Sokoto on the Rima River. It is a large Hausa village made exclusively of mud bricks on a rocky outcrop overlooking the river. Its claim to fame is the tomb of Sultan Bello.

Zaria

General

Zaria is one of the original walled Hausa cities, founded in the 16th century. It is an attractive city which has retained its ancient looks to some degree by leaving most of the modern development and industry to Kaduna nearby! It was once surrounded by approximately 19 km of walls which in some areas are well-preserved. The Zaria area used to be part of the ancient kingdom of Zazzia, but it was renamed Zaria in honour of the chief's wife. Zaria has 2 important establishments: the Ahmadu Bello University at Samaru on the Sokoto road, founded in 1962, which was the first university in the north of the country, and the Regimental Depot of the Nigerian Army on Kaduna Road. The depot has the Regimental Museum of the Nigerian Army. Zaria has a splendid Sallah, especially at *Id-el-Fitri*. The old town has many very decorative buildings, including the Emir's palace and the central mosque (a replica of which can be seen in the Museum of Architecture at Jos). Some traditional crafts are still carried on in Zaria, and it is possible to see the blacksmiths and the potters at work.

Route

Zaria old town is to the right of the main Kaduna - Kano road. (For directions from Lagos to Kaduna, see page 81.) If you go into the town you will not be disappointed.

We invite you to experience Paradise ...in Abuja

The Royal Weekend

From Friday to Sunday, it's Royal treatment all the way.
Get away from the hustle and bustle to the peace and comfort of the luxurious NICON NOGA HILTON HOTEL. Relax and enjoy our extensive recreational facilities. Indulge in our excellent national and international cuisine, and explore the beauty of Abuja. Come for a weekend that is truly royal. It's like being in Paradise.

NICON-NOGA HILTON HOTEL ABUJA
Let's spoil you a little

For reservation please call: Tel: [09] 5231811 to 828 Telex: 71504 HILTON NG P.M.B 200, Abuja, F.C.T., Nigeria.
Lagos Office: Plot 1620, Danmole Street, Victoria Island. Tel: 618997.

EXCEL

The symbol of excellence

Excel, the choice cigarette for people who appreciate quality and cherish excellence.
Excel Filter Cigarette, blended from the finest tobaccos.

 Makers of Nigeria's finest cigarettes   Price: ₦4.50k for 20

Give your wheels the *ELITE* feeling...

Drive DUNLOP ELITE TYRES

Get the elite feeling on wheels. Drive Dunlop ELITE, the new generation of tyres. Years of development went into the Elite Series. Computer-aided design, sophisticated laboratory testing and thousands of hours on road and track have produced a tyre to provide kilometre after kilometre of economical motoring. Specifically designed for safety, and durability, the Elite series offers value for money that is difficult to match. It's available in a range of three tyre sizes for cars and vans.
Go the elite way, drive DUNLOP ELITE.

1. Wide tread shoulder grooves for rapid water dispersal.
2. Three pitch sequences for low road noise.
3. Knife cuts for improved wet grip.
4. 'Zigzag' block edges for improved tread wear.
5. Large tread blocks for stable handling.

- 165 SR13 Elite
- 175 SR14 ,,
- 185 SR14 ,,

Prices from ₦377.00k

– Safety on Wheels

Hotels

Zaria is only an hour's journey north of Kaduna. So it is probably best to use the hotels in Kaduna (see page 82, but there is also *The Conference Hotel,* at Kongo, near the university.

Zuma Rock

The Zuma Rock is one of the natural landmarks of Nigeria. It is an enormous inselberg or granite rock, standing out from the surrounding countryside like a giant stone altar. It even has the semblance of a face etched on it when you approach it from the south. The rock itself is about 1 km long and several hundred metres high, with sheer rock faces on all sides carved into vertical lines by centuries of heavy rainfall running down from the summit in the wet season. It makes a spectacular photograph. A hotel is being constructed at the foot of the rock, which hopefully will not intrude upon the view. The rock can be seen on the right soon after you pass the northern turn-off to Abuja (the dual carriageway) on the A2 road between Lokoja and Kaduna. It cannot be mistaken for any other inselberg.

Zungeru

General

Zungeru was Lord Lugard's northern capital. There are still a few signs of his occupation left, including the old bridge across a tributary of the Kaduna River, the old garrison church, some war-graves and the ruins of some buildings. We were informed that it was only possible to see the ruins properly in the dry season, as at the time we wanted to visit them, the grass was too high. This is not a tourist site, but it is of interest to historians. If you are passing that way there is a scenic bridge across the Kaduna River which passes through a gorge with curious rock formations. The old bridge is shared by motor vehicles and the railway, which is somewhat unusual, but a new road-bridge was opened at the end of 1989 a few kilometres further north on the

Tegina - Minna road The direct route no longer goes through Zungeru. There are plans to dam the Kaduna River near Zungeru. If these plans are carried out, Zungeru may change from a quiet town, to that of a bustling industrial area.

Route

Zungeru is on the old Minna - Tegina road in Niger State. There are no hotels in the town, but see page 88 on Minna. To reach the historical sites, coming from Minna on the old road, turn right in the centre of the town off the main road, and it is another 1-2 km further on, across the small bridge on a tributary of the Kaduna River. We found an elderly man who acted as our guide and was very helpful.

5
North-East

Introduction

General

North-east Nigeria is the area north of the Benue River, bordered in the north and east by the countries of Niger, Cameroon and Chad, and in the west by the state boundaries of Kano and Kaduna. It includes the states of Plateau, Bauchi, Borno and the northern part of Gongola State. It, therefore, has such sharply contrasting landscapes as the picturesque Jos Plateau which rises to over 1,219 m, the Mandara Mountains running down the border with Cameroon, and the flat, low-lying, Lake Chad basin. Many

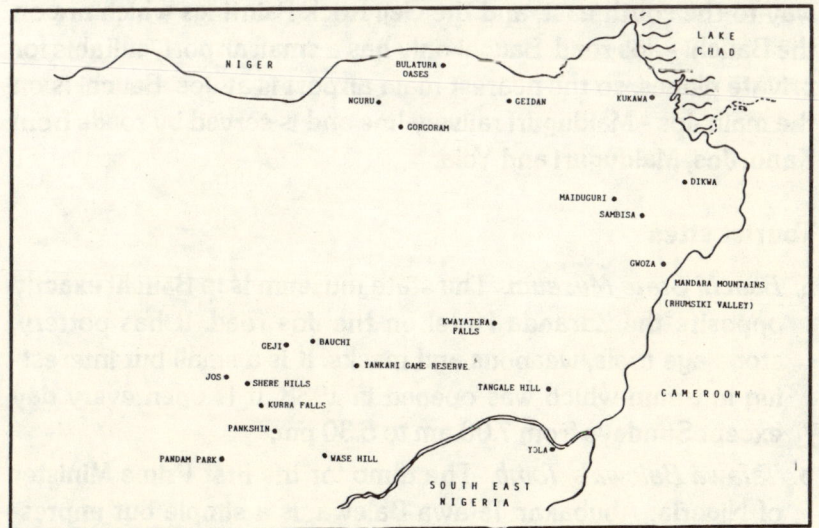

centuries ago, when Lake Chad was a great deal larger, much of the north-east corner of Borno was under the waters of the lake. The north-east also includes the wetlands of Hadejia-Nguru. In the far north of Borno State there are the ever-encroaching sands of the Sahara desert. One can see rolling dunes and oases. The people are of many tribes and religions, although they are predominantly muslim, but this region is sparsely populated in comparison with the south. Because of the distance, it is not often visited by people from Lagos, except for well-known places like Jos and the Yankari Game Reserve. For this reason, many of the tourist sites are undeveloped, but the area should not be neglected by the keen traveller, as it has much to offer, and has some of the most scenic areas in Nigeria.

Bauchi

General

Bauchi town is the fast-growing capital of Bauchi State. It is surrounded by some attractive hills, and can be used as a base to visit both the Yankari Game Reserve, which is about $1\frac{1}{2}$ hours away to the south-east, and the Geji Rock Paintings which are on the Bauchi - Jos road. Bauchi only has a small airport, suitable for private planes, so the nearest main airport is at Jos. Bauchi is on the main Jos - Maiduguri railway line and is served by roads from Kano, Jos, Maiduguri and Yola.

Tourist sites

a. *Bauchi State Museum.* The state museum is in Bauchi exactly opposite the Zaranda Hotel on the Jos road. It has pottery, stone age tools, weapons and masks. It is a small but interesting museum which was opened in 1988. It is open every day except Sundays from 7.00 am to 5.30 pm.

b. *Tafawa Balewa's Tomb.* The tomb for the first Prime Minister of Nigeria, Abubakar Tafawa Balewa, is a simple but impressive monument. Behind it is a historical section with a library showing videos of Independence Day and some of the personal effects of the late Prime Minister, who left this earth with very little he could call his own apart from his small family farm. The memorial to this great man epitomises his simple, dedicated and loyal life as a teacher, prime minister and leader of Nigeria until he was killed in Nigeria's first coup. The tomb is at Ran Road, (Old Maiduguri Road), Bauchi. It is open from 8.00 am to 6.00 pm from Monday to Friday and from 8.00 am to 12.00 pm on Saturdays.

Route

The best route to Bauchi is Lagos - Ajaokuta (the new bridge across the Niger) - Makurdi - Jos - Bauchi.

Hotels

The *Zaranda Hotel* can be clearly seen on the right, coming from Jos, shortly before entering the town. It is a tall cream-coloured building close to the road. It is a modern hotel with a swimming pool, and has an excellent view of the surrounding countryside. There is a Yankari booking office in the reception hall. Tel: (077) 42480. There is also the *Awalah Hotel* on the junction of the roads to Kano and Kari a few kilometres north of Bauchi, which is less expensive than the Zaranda.

Bulatura Oases

The Bulatura Oases are on the western side of Borno State, north-east of Nguru. The area is the 'desert' of the Hollywood film - set dunes, camels, and palm trees around an oasis. To visit this area, it is necessary to have a 4-wheel drive vehicle which is prepared for operating in such conditions, and essential to have a guide, but the area is most attractive, and an experience for those who have not been in the desert before. The oases are also excellent for bird-watchers and in the dry season there are thousands of palaearctic migrants wintering there. The Project Officer at the headquarters of the Hadejia-Nguru Wetlands Project in Nguru, could advise you. (See page 108 on Nguru). There is no modern hotel at Nguru, but basic accommodation is available at either the *Nguru Guest Inn* or *the Green Garden Hotel.* Although the accommodation is better at the former, the food is reputed to be better at the latter. It is also possible to camp either at the Project Headquarters, with the permission of the Project Officer, or at the Oases themselves. From Nguru, the first part of the route is along the Maiduguri road, until you reach the village of Jajimaji. From here, the road is a sandy track all the way to the Oases which is over an hour's journey. As stated earlier, a guide is necessary as there are many tracks. It would be easy to lose one's way. This trip is only recommended for the traveller who is used to rugged conditions.

Dikwa

Dikwa, in Borno State, was where the Shehu (King) of Dikwa, a marauder from the Sudan, lived at the beginning of this century. There is an interesting mudbrick fort in the town which is being restored by the National Museum. The Shehu's tomb is nearby, but has not yet been restored. The fort is chiefly of interest to historians, and there is a small but colourful market in the village where you can see Kanuri women with their decorative hairstyles. The old German DC's house is still standing. Dikwa is about one hour's drive due east of Maiduguri along the A3 which is a good road. The surrounding landscape is a flat, barren, thornbush country, and camel-trains are not an unusual sight.

Geidam

Geidam is in the very north of Borno State, north-west of Maiduguri, and is an old desert city which has seen better days. Nearby is the old city of Birnin N'Gazargamo which was the capital of Borno at the beginning of the 19th century. It was sacked by the Fulani jihadists and is now only a ruin of scattered bricks. The route to Geidam from Maiduguri is north via Gubio. A few kilometres before Damasak the road becomes a sandy track and from there to Geidam it is only possible in a 4-wheel drive vehicle, with a guide, as it is a poorly defined desert track. It is recommended for the adventurous traveller.

Geji Rock Paintings

The Geji rock paintings are at Dutseen Sare near Geji in Bauchi State, on the Bauchi - Jos road. The paintings are like those at Birnin Kudu (see page 77), not all that clear nor particularly large or impressive. However, they are of interest to historians, because they are almost certainly very old. There is a red sign on the left of the main road about 30 km from Bauchi. If coming from Jos, the red sign is on the right close to the 472 km stone to Maiduguri. A track leads to the right (coming from Bauchi) off the main road northwards for $6\frac{1}{2}$ Km to the settlement of Dutseen Sare. From here the local boys will guide you, for a suitable sum, the $1\frac{1}{2}$ km to the Geji inselberg where you will see a caged area protecting the paintings.

This area is also notable for its women who extend their lips by placing coins or round objects in them, but never photograph the women without first asking their permission. The best base for a visit to Geji is either Jos or Bauchi, but Bauchi is the nearest.

Gorgoram

Gorgoram is the old walled town which was once the capital of the Bade Emirate. It lies in the middle of the Hadejia wetlands surrounded by 'fadama' which host thousands of birds. A good contact is the primary school teacher who may find you a guide, or ask for the Forestry/Wildlife staff. If you are based in Nguru, the NCF representative at the Hadejia-Nguru Wetlands Project could advise you on the state of the roads, etc. The only way to get there is through Gashua, on the route between Nguru and Maiduguri. From Gashua take a minor road in a south-west direction.

Gwoza Hills

Gwoza is south-east of Maiduguri on the main road to Yola. The hills to the south and east of Gwoza along the Cameroon border are very scenic, and there is a fortified town south of Mabgali called Sukor, about 25 km south of Gwoza. Ask in the area for directions. Sukor is very interesting, as, in addition to the fortifications, it is one of the few places where the people smelt their own iron to make tools, as filmed by the Basil Davidson 'Africa' team. It is about $1\frac{1}{2}$ hours walk up a remarkable stone-built 'pathway'. From Gwoza, there is a shorter walk/climb into the hills from the valley behind the town, which goes to the village of Guduf, where there are interesting 'bone' huts. Park by the primary school in the valley.

Jos

General

Jos has always been a popular place with Europeans because of its height above sea level, (1,219 m), cool evenings, unique rocky scenery of the plateau and many tourist sites to visit. It is the capital of Plateau State and is served by roads going north, south, east and west, by the railway and an airport. It has 2 golf courses, Rayfield and Plateau, a Polo club and numerous other forms of sport and entertainment. Jos used to be an important tin mining centre, and mining can be observed at Bukuru to the south of the city.

Tourist sites

a. *National Museum, Museum of Architecture and Zoo.* The National Museum in Jos is one of the best in Nigeria, especially for archaeology and pottery. It has many fine examples of Nok heads and artefacts, which were discovered in Plateau State and date from between 500 BC and 200 AD. The Pottery Hall has an exceptionally good collection of pots from all over the country. The museum of architecture is in the same grounds and is on the right as you drive into the museum car park. It contains life-size replicas of the different forms of Nigerian architecture, from the walls of Kano to the Mosque at Zaria and a Tiv village. The Zoo is next to the National Museum and is of interest to children. The museum is in the residential area, quite close to the Hill Station Hotel. Ask for directions from the hotel staff.

b. *Jos Wildlife Park.* The wildlife park does not compare with similar parks in Europe or America, but it is attractively set out and of interest to those who enjoy seeing animals, and of course, to children. It is 8 sq. km of unspoilt savannah bush, and the rare pigmy hippopotamus is successfully being bred here in a 'hippo pool'. The lions are in a large enclosure simulating their natural habitat, and there are elephants, a red river hog, jackal, a chimpanzee, monkeys, crocodiles and other animals. There is a watch-tower at the top of Vong Nfwei Hill, the highest point in the Park (1,345 m) with an excellent view of Jos and the surrounding area, where it would be possible to picnic, but the road up to it is not in very good condition. However, apart from the park, there are caged animals near the offices, which you can visit on foot. The park opens at 10.00 am. and the charges are minimal. The route to the Park from the Hill Station Hotel is as follows: take the dual carriageway towards Bukuru and after passing the very obvious red and white Nasco factory on your left, you will see Miango Road on your right, signed to the Park. After travelling 4 km, you will see the entrance to the Park on your right.

c. *The Shere Hills.* The Shere Hills are the hills that can be seen to the east of Jos. One way of getting to the hills is to turn right off the eastern bypass to Bauchi, where it curves to the left, bear right (east) up towards the Plateau Golf Club, and continue on into the hills. It is a scenic area for walks and picnics. Go prepared with plenty of water, haversack rations and good walking shoes. As always when walking in the 'bush', take careful note of your route! For more details of the area, seek local advice.

d. *Jos Ultra-Modern Market.* The Jos market is a purpose-built modern market with 4,290 stalls, car park and other services such as banks and a post office. The market is worth a visit. It is on the Bauchi road, in the centre of the town just below the residential area.

e. *Naraguta Leatherworks and Pottery.* At Naraguta village near the Jos University ladies hostel on the Bauchi road is the Naraguta Leatherworks and Pottery where leather articles and decorative pots can be bought. It is signed to the left off the Bauchi road a few kilometres from Jos.

Jos, as a centre for tourism, has much to offer in the surrounding area, all within a day's drive there and back.

Other Tourist sites

a. *Assop Falls.* This is a small waterfall, (best seen in the wet season) which could make a pleasant picnic spot on a drive from Jos to Abuja, about 64 km from Jos. It is a few kilometres before Gimi, (the turn-off to Akwanga and Abuja), and is signed on the right of the road after descending a steep hill from the plateau. There is a parking area, off the road, and a small charge for entry.

b. *Riyom Rock.* This pile of rocks is a photographer's dream. It is a dramatic pile of rocks balanced on top of one another, with one looking like a clown's hat, perched precariously on the top. The rocks can be seen on the main Jos-Gimi road on the right, coming from Jos. After passing by Bukuru and Vom, the road drops between embankments to cross a bridge. Soon afterwards you will see this strange pile of rocks on your right near a village with cactus hedges - a typical feature of this area.

c. *Kurra Falls.* This is a very pleasant area for walks and picnics, with scenery similar to the Scottish highlands. It is south-west of Jos on the road towards Panyam. See page 105.

d. *Wase Rock or Hill.* This is an impressive inselberg which rises 250 m above the plateau with sheer sides. It is 43 km east of Langtang and 216 km from Jos (see page 112).

e. *Pandam Wildlife Park.* This is a rather undeveloped game reserve between Shendam and Lafia on the right of the road. It is approximately 300 km from Jos (see page 109).

There are a number of projects planned for tourists around Jos, but as at 1989 they had not been completed. They are the Mado Tourist village, close to the Jos Wildlife Park; the Health Resort at Kerang springs, and the Rock Hotel at Liberty Dam.

Route

The best route from Lagos is via Abuja then to Akwanga, Gimi and Jos, but it is a 2-day journey. The best advice is to have an overnight stop at the Abuja Hilton which is a day's drive, leaving only a morning's journey for the second day. From Kaduna there are 2 routes, the northern, A11, or the southern route, A235, via Kachia and Kagoro. The northern route is the shortest but the southern route is the more scenic. Both roads had good surfaces in late 1989.

Hotels

Jos has 2 modern hotels, the *Hill Station Hotel*, 10 Tudun Wada Road, Tel: (073) 55300-2, 52808, 54817, and the *Plateau Hotel*, 2 Rest House Road, Tel: (073) 55740. Both are in the centre of the residential area of Jos, on high ground overlooking the town. The Hill Station Hotel had a new annex opened in 1988, and is the recommended of the two. For those who wish to eat out, the *Andulusia Restaurant*, which is Lebanese owned, has been recommended. It is on the right of the dual carriageway going towards Bukuru.

Kukawa

General

Kukawa is a town close to Lake Chad in Borno State. Its only claim to fame is the tomb of El-Kanemi, the warrior who, on two occasions, assisted the Mai (King) of Borno to quell the Fulani uprisings and then undertook military campaigns around the kingdom of Borno to stop the Fulani from winning back Borno's former vassals and make safe the borders of the kingdom. El-Kanemi was also a Muslim scholar who adhered strictly to the faith, a skilful diplomat and a clever politician. He was the founder of the Shehu (Kanemi) dynasty in Borno and built his new capital at Kukawa in 1814. He died in 1835. There is not a great deal left of the tomb to see, but it is an interesting and historical area to visit.

Route

From Maiduguri the direct road to Monguna has been rehabilitated so you do not have to go via Dikwa. From Monguna take the road north to Kauwa then turn left to Kukawa. If you wish to do the round trip back to Maiduguri, there is a good road to Damasak, but there is no accommodation there. For the first few kilometres from Damasak to Gubio the road becomes a sandy track, but most of the way to Maiduguri, it is good tarmac. It would be wise to take up-to-date advice about the state of these roads before leaving Maiduguri.

Kurra Falls

General

The Kurra Falls themselves can only be seen in the wet season when there is plenty of water, as they do not exist in the dry season. However, the surrounding is very scenic in the dry season and is a pleasant picnic or camping spot. The author camped there in 1980, and greatly enjoyed the splendid views of typical 'Scottish' scenery with hills, lakes and moors. The area is the property of NESCO, an electrical company whose head office is in Bukuru, near Jos. The Kurra Falls area is very attractive, has fine walks and a variety of birdlife. If you have time during a visit to Jos, do not miss this day's outing.

Route

From Jos take the main road south and at the roundabout take the Pankshin road to Barakin Ladi (24 km from the roundabout). Fork right off the main road at a sign reading 'Kurra Falls'. Pass the General Hospital on your left, drive on for 3 km and turn right at another sign to the falls. Drive another 27 km along a good road to Kurra Falls village. Report to the NESCO office on the right, or if that is closed, to the police for permission to enter the area. Ask for a guide if you want to see the falls, otherwise proceed through the village taking a left fork until you meet a barrier where you turn right and cross a bridge on the outskirts of the village. Drive on up the road to another barrier, which is manned by a NESCO employee. The road continues for a further 10 km from the village, past the reservoirs. You can stop and choose your ideal picnic spot somewhere along this road.

Kwayatera Waterfall

The Kwayatera waterfall is about 30 km from Biu on the Gombe to Biu road, east of Bauchi. It is best visited during the wet season, say July to September, when there will be plenty of water running. As you drive south from Biu, look for the signboard pointing to the irrigation scheme and also for the track to the right. Take this track and turn left to the waterfall before you reach the irrigation scheme. Park at the top of the fall, and the path to the bottom is downstream.

Lake Chad Area

Lake Chad would appear on the map as a huge expanse of water - one imagines plenty of fishing boats and bird and animal life in abundance. But due to the recent droughts, Lake Chad has shrunk considerably and the Nigerian part of the lake consists mostly of marshes. However, as a result of heavy rains there was again some water in the lake in 1989 and the bird-life returned in large numbers. It would be wise to take up-to-date advice from the headquarters of the Lake Chad Development Authority in Maiduguri or from Baba Grema, Chief Wildlife Officer in the Forestry Department in the State Secretariat, before attempting to visit the area. They can advise you of the route via Baga which is some kilometres from the lake along a canal, but the distance varies enormously with the level of water in the lake. From Maiduguri, the first part of the route is via Dikwa and Monguno. For the best route to Maiduguri see page 107.

Mandara Mountains (See Rhumsiki Valley on page 111).

Maiduguri
General

Maiduguri is the capital of Borno State in the far north-east of the country and is served by an airport. It is at the end of the railway line from Port Harcourt and has 5 main roads leading from it. It is also a base for a visit to northern Cameroon, but remember to get your visas in Lagos or Calabar, as there is no Consular Office for the Cameroons in Maiduguri. It is a pleasant city with wide roads, tree-lined avenues and interesting roundabouts.

The main tourist attraction is the Kyarimi Park which has one of the best zoos in Nigeria and is a pleasant, shady place to visit. The animals include a small herd of eland, several elephants, a hippopotamus and a large number of crocodiles. The zoo is frequented by many wild birds, attracted by the food for the animals. This is an added bonus. About 200 m from the entrance to the zoo, there is a row of handicraft stalls selling leather goods and other local crafts.

Tourist sites

Borno State Museum. The museum was commissioned in 1984. It is quite small, but well laid out and interesting. It has displays of arms, armour, pottery, baskets, mats, jewellery and household items. It is very much a museum for those interested in the local culture and people. The museum is close to the Customs roundabout, Maiduguri, near the junction of Sir Kashim Ibrahim Road, Gambaru Road and Bama Road, and is signed. There are several places of interest to visit nearby, including Dikwa, (see page 98) and the Sambisa Game Reserve (see page 111). Many of the local people are Kanuris, who are unique in their mode of dressing, hairstyles and tradition - a further example of the fascinating diversity of cultures in Nigeria.

Route

The best route from Lagos is via Abuja - Jos - Bauchi - Gombe - Biu - Maiduguri, but it is a 3-day drive, so it is much quicker to fly. However, it would be a pity to miss the interesting change of scenery from rainforest to semi-desert en route. It is advisable to go by road if you can spare the time.

Hotels

Maiduguri has 2 reasonable hotels: the *Deribe* and the *Lake Chad Hotel* (not to be confused with the Lake Chad Club). The Deribe does not sell alcohol (due to Muslim religious tenets), but is recommended of the two. Both have swimming pools. The Lake Chad Hotel is in Sir Kashim Ibrahim Road, Tel: (076) 232400, 231869, and the Deribe is nearby, just off the main dual carriageway, near the 'catfish' roundabout. Tel 231662. (Again, do not confuse this with the Deribe Motel on Kano road). There is a Chinese Restaurant close to the Deribe Hotel which serves good Chinese and Nigerian food.

Nguru

General

Nguru is in the north-west of Borno State, close to the border with Kano State. It is an old trading and market town with strong links northwards into Niger. It is of special interest to keen ornithologists, because it is the headquarters of the Hadejia-Nguru Wetlands Conservation Project. This is a project funded by the Royal Society for the Protection of Birds (RSPB), ICBP, the IUCN and the NCF, not only to preserve the wetlands as a viable agricultural area but also as a reserve for indigenous birds and the many species of palaearctic birds that seek sanctuary in Africa from the harsh European winter. During the dry season, it is home to many thousands of ducks, waders and other water birds.

Tourist sites

The *Dagona Wildfowl Sanctuary* was opened by the Duke of Edinburgh in 1989. It is an excellent place to see a wide variety of water birds including several varieties of ibis, duck, geese, waders and pelicans. To reach it, take the Gashua (Maiduguri) road out of Nguru and after approximately 32 km, it is signed to the right. Take the sandy track for approximately 15 km until you reach

Zuma Rock near Abuja

Flower of the Baobab tree *(Adansonia digitata)*

Rocks near Gwoza

Riyom Rocks near Jos

Kamale Pinnacle, Mandara Mountains

Camel in semi-desert sahel zone, Nguru

Lioness in Yankari Game Reserve

Wikki Warm Springs, Yankari Game Reserve

the lakes. The route takes you through a village, and it would be courteous to ask for permission, and if necessary a guide, to visit the sanctuary.

Near Nguru it is possible to see the attractive local mats being made. They were woven from dum palm in hollowed out underground chambers, as it is too dry to make them on the surface. Ask for directions in the town. Nguru can also be used as a base to visit Gorgoram (see page 99), Geidam (page 98) or the Bulatura and other oases (page 97). There is an interesting Saturday market at Jajimaji, some 40 km along the Maiduguri Road, where it is possible to buy the colourful mats described above, made from palm leaves.

Route

The shortest route from Kano, a 3-hour journey, is via Gezawa, Gujungu and Hadejia. From Bauchi the route is via Potiskum - Gashua - Nguru.

Hotels

There are 2 small hotels with very basic facilities: the *Nguru Guest Inn* and the *Green Garden Hotel*. The first is considered more up-market but the food at the latter is reputed to be better. It might be possible to get accommodation at the HQ of the Project if you know someone in the NCF to arrange it, and you are prepared to have meals at the Green Garden Hotel. It might also be possible to camp at the Project HQ if you can get permission. However, there are some excellent government guest houses in Nguru if your visit is an official one.

Pandam Wildlife Park

General

Pandam Wildlife Park is not yet fully-developed by Plateau State Government. The wildlife reserve is 140 sq. km in size and has a beautiful natural lake, with a shady picnic spot. It is possible to organise a boat trip on the lake (we went out in a boat with a somewhat dodgy outboard motor!). It is a large, scenic lake, surrounded by tall trees, and we saw hippos in the distance and baboons along the shore. There are manatees in the lake, brought from the Jos Wildlife Park, but they are unlikely to be seen. There are many different species of birds and we watched an Osprey fishing. We also saw a rare Long-toed lapwing. You can also hire a guide to escort you in your vehicle round the park, but you may not see elephants or lions.

Route

The best route to Pandam from either Abuja or Jos is to go via Akwanga then to Lafia; turn right towards Shendam and approximately 57 km from Lafia the wildlife park is signed on the left of the road. The office and chalets can be seen from the road.

Hotels

There are about 15-20 small chalets, with a restaurant in the park. The chalets have no shade, no air-conditioners and the generator only goes on at 6.00 pm. However, if one were prepared with a camping stove and food, it would be possible to semi-camp there at present, but the State Government intends to developing it further. It is within reach of a long day-trip from either Jos (via Akwanga) or Abuja. The *Lafia Hotel,* on the right of the Shendam road just outside Lafia town, could be a possible overnight stop.

Pankshin

Pankshin is 120 km south-east of Jos on the Jos Plateau, 30 km from Panyam. The *Pankshin Hotel* is set on a hill with fine views of the surrounding hills and is said to be quite reasonable. The town is known for its pottery, especially for its pots which taper at the bottom. It is a very attractive area with many panoramic views, excellent walks and scenic drives.

Rhumsiki Valley

The Rhumsiki Valley is an area of impressive inselbergs in the Mandara Mountain range, north-east of Mubi in the very north of Gongola State, along the Cameroon border. The area has fantastic volcanic plugs standing up like giant pillars from the surrounding rugged countryside. One of the well-known peaks in the area is the Kamale Pinnacle, featured in Peter Holmes's book, *Nigeria, Giant of Africa*. It is like an enormous finger pointing towards the sky. Either Yola or Maiduguri might be used as a base. To obtain a good view of the Kamale pinnacle, go to the village of Michika on the way from Yola, mid-way between Yola and Maiduguri, turn right (east) at the sign saying 'Government Junior Secondary School, Garta', and continue on the laterite track for several kilometres until you can get a good view of the pinnacle. The first part of the track is suitable for ordinary cars, but further on, a 4-wheel drive vehicle is essential. Remember that this area is very close to the border, and you may be required to prove your identity.

Shere Hills

See Jos page 100

Sambisa Game Reserve

The Sambisa Game Reserve is included in this guide for those who are interested in the flora and fauna of the far north-east of the country. The reserve is south-east of Maiduguri towards Bama, to the right of the road. It is not marked, and, therefore, it is absolutely necessary to have a guide. If you wish to visit this area, contact the Chief Wildlife Officer in the Forestry Department in the State Secretariat in Maiduguri or one of his assistants. They will be willing to help you. The reserve has big game including elephants and many birds like ostriches, marabou storks, tawny eagles and the magnificent bateleur. We were lucky enough to see a secretary bird. The reserve has no accommodation or facilities, but is within easy reach of Maiduguri.

Tangale Hill

Tangale Hill in Bauchi State can be seen quite clearly from the road when you drive from Gombe towards Numan. The hill is a volcanic plug and can be climbed with a guide after getting permission from the Emir of Kaltungo. The climb is said to take about 3 hours. The area is good for walking. The best base is either Bauchi or Yola. No doubt, some accommodation could be found in Gombe or Numan, e.g. a company guest house, but there are no modern hotels in either place. There is a Catering Rest House in Gombe, but we have not visited it.

Wase Hill

Wase Hill or Rock, as it is sometimes called, in Plateau State, is a remarkable rock rising 250 m perpendicularly out of the surrounding area. It is chiefly of interest to geologists and mountain climbers, but the rock has many legends surrounding it. One of them is that an emir was said to have offered a reprieve to 2 murderers if they climbed to the top. One fell on the way up and was killed, the other reached the top but died of exhaustion. The rock was climbed in 1959 by a Mr P T Wallace, who planted the flag of the Emir of Wase on the summit. Another expedition led by a Mr Wilkinson ended in disaster when a swarm of bees attacked the climbing team, and he was unfortunately stung to death. A game reserve has recently been declared around the rock to protect its fauna. It is reputed that Pelicans used to nest on the rock, but this has not been recently authenticated. The route from Jos is south-east to Panyam, east to Pankshin (see page 110) and Amper, south to Langtang, then finally south-east to Wase, which is approximately 220 km from Jos and 100 km from Pankshin.

Yankari Game Reserve

General

Yankari Game Reserve and the Wikki Warm Springs are approximately $1\frac{1}{2}$ hours drive south-east of Bauchi. The reserve is the best in Nigeria, but does not compare with the facilities at game reserves in East Africa. There is much work to be done on accommodation, water supply, electricity, the restaurant and other essential facilities to bring it up to international tourist standards. However, in spite of this, it is well worth a visit, particularly if you know what to expect and are not looking for luxury!

The game reserve was set up in 1956 and was opened to the public in 1962. It is based around the Gagi River which is the main game-viewing area. It is open all the year although in the wet season some of the tracks are impassable. The best time of the year to visit is from November to May, but the closer you are to the end of the dry season the more game you are likely to see, as the vegetation has died down and the animals concentrate arround the river. Even so, game-viewing trips can be very variable - one morning we saw practically nothing, yet in the evening of the same day large numbers of birds and animals were on show. Game runs are generally better in the evening as the game come down to the river to drink after the heat of the day.

The *warm springs* at Wikki Camp are one of the best features of the game reserve. They are flood-lit at night, and it is wonderful, after a hot day's game-viewing to relax in the warm water. The spring gushes out from under a cliff, where the water is at least 2 m deep, and the bathing area extends for about 200 m to a large sandy beach. Beware of the baboons, who may steal your clothing and valuables unless you keep a look-out. They have also been known to get into chalets and cars to steal food, and can be dangerous, so take care of young children, especially. They are extremely cunning animals.

The animals that are most often seen in the reserve are elephant, baboon, waterbuck, bushbuck, duiker, oribi, crocodile, hippopotamus, roan antelope, buffalo and warthog (although both the latter species are less common since an epidemic of rinderpest killed many of them), and various types of monkeys. Lions are occasionally seen, but they are so well-camouflaged that in seven visits we have only seen them once. The birds are many and varied, including the huge saddlebill stork, goliath heron, bateleur eagle, fish eagle, vultures, kingfishers, bee-eaters, etc. So it is excellent for keen bird-watchers. You can either go game-viewing in the Yankari transport, or take your own car with a guide, but a 4-wheel drive is advisable, as some of the roads are badly maintained. The tsetse fly can be a nuisance, so take some insect repellent. Always take plenty of water on these trips, because if the car breaks down, you must wait in the vehicle until the guide obtains help, which could take some time.

It is not particularly cheap to visit Yankari as there are entrance fees to pay at the entrance to the park, (about 43 km from Wikki Camp), and charges for the use of cameras, especially video cameras, and with a family the charges can mount up. The entrance fees are higher for weekends and public holidays. There is no charge for the use of the warm springs, unless you are a day visitor, but this is minimal. It is better to book game runs in advance when you arrive, to ensure that there will be a guide available.

There are tennis courts and a squash court for the sports enthusiast, and a small museum in the reception area. There is a Mobil petrol pump at Wikki Camp, but do not rely upon it; fill up with petrol in Bauchi.

Bookings. It is advisable to book for holidays and weekends, and Easter is a particularly popular time. You can either book at the Zaranda Hotel in Bauchi or send a courier letter to Yankari Game Reserve. The most reliable method, as always, is to ask a friend who is going there before you, to make your booking - but how often does this happen when you need it?

Route

The best route from Lagos is via Abuja where you can make an overnight stop, and then to Jos and Bauchi, as it is a 2-day journey by car. From Bauchi take the Gombe road (towards Yola). After approximately 40 km, you cross a bridge over the Gongola River. Turn right at the sign to Yankari Game Reserve almost immediately after crossing the bridge, through the village of Dindima. Wikki Camp is 72 km from the main road, although the entrance to the park is reached after about 30 km. The road to the camp has broken up in 1990 and unless repaired is badly potholed. The roads within the park when you go on game-viewing runs are entirely laterite and are rough in places.

Hotels

The accommodation is in chalets or rondavels and is rather basic. It is advisable to inspect your rooms before accepting them. There is no electricity during the day, thus no water until 6.00 pm when the generator is turned on. However, if you keep the buckets in the bathroom full this is no great problem. The Wikki Warm Springs are so close you can have a swim instead of a shower. The types of accommodation are as follows:

    Super suite
    VIP suite   (Recommended)
    Special double   (Recommended)
    Family Chalet
    Old Double

The restaurant is variable, but we were able to get simple but acceptable food for dinner on our last visit. It is advisabe to take some of your own food, especially tins, breakfast cereals and snacks for picnics. There is a small shop in the camp which sells a few items of food, and there is a bar for beer and soft drinks, but these are not always open.

6

Across-Border Travel

BENIN REPUBLIC

CAMEROON

MALI

NIGER

TOGO

General Introduction

This chapter is designed for the traveller who wishes to travel outside Nigeria and see the neighbouring countries of West Africa, but is confined to those places that are within reasonable driving distance of Nigeria. It is impossible to make this a comprehensive guide, but it will cover important information such as the route from Lagos, documentation, the major attractions, and one or two hotels. After that it is up to you either to see a travel agent or to go to the embassy of the country you are hoping to visit for more information. Apologies if the information is not up to date, but the guide will help you to assess if the country has places that are likely to be of interest to you. We have travelled to many of the places, and have read tourist brochures and enquired of our fellow-travellers for additional information. This, we believe, would be a good basis from which you can plan your tours.

BENIN (DAHOMEY) REPUBLIC
Cotonou
General
Cotonou, the largest town in Benin (pronounced Be-ne), or Dahomey as it was earlier called, is only about 3 hours from Lagos. The country has many similarities with Nigeria, but the difference is that Benin has a background of French culture. Therefore, there are excellent restaurants and some good hotels. Porto Novo is the capital of Benin and the centre of government, but Cotonou has more attractions for the tourist.

Benin is very sensitive about photography so do not photograph anything that might cause trouble, like military establishments, government buildings, airports, docks, bridges, etc. As in Nigeria, ask before taking a photograph. Please remember that the sea can be very dangerous with a severe undertow. Do not assume the water is safe because you see others swimming. It is only 'safe' on calm days and even then care must be taken, especially with children. Use the hotel pool, just to be sure of your family's safety.

Tourist sites
a. The Dan Tokpa market situated beside the lagoon near the new bridge.
b. Cotonou Cathedral with its red and white exterior.
c. Handicrafts market near the old bridge.
d. Fishing harbour and the old wharf.

Route

Leave Lagos by going past the National Theatre and getting onto the Badagry expressway. This is a fast dual carriageway except near Lagos where there can be traffic jams. It takes about $1\frac{1}{2}$ hours to get to the border. If you are going on to Togo or touring Benin, fill up your tank well before the border, because the border pumps are often dry. Once you reach Cotonou, go straight through the town past the President's Palace until the dual carriageway gives way to single line traffic and another kilometre brings you to the Sheraton Hotel. Door to door from Lagos your journey should only take about $2\frac{1}{2}$ to 3 hours, but this very much depends upon the border procedure, which can be lengthy. It varies according to the time of day, the number of people in your car, etc, but plan to spend between 30 minutes to 1 hour to cross the border.

Hotels

There is no shortage of hotels in Cotonou for all tastes. They include the *Hotel de la Plage* and *Croix du Sud,* but I would recommend the *Sheraton.* They do a special 'package' over the weekend, Friday to Monday, and provide bed & breakfast, a 'welcome' drink and a fruit basket. You can use credit cards and all normally recognised cards seem to be acceptable. The hotel is relatively modern and is 4 to 5 star standard. There are numerous restaurants in Cotonou if you do not want to eat in the hotel. Some places like the *Paris Snack* or *Restaurant Edelweiss,* and *La Verdure* are highly recommended, but there are others if you look around. Do not drive past the President's Palace after dark, as it is closed at night, and there are armed guards. There is a tourist village called *PLM Hotel Alefo* which is said to have a safe beach. It is 3 km from the centre of Cotonou, but the standard of the hotel is not known.

Travel documents

The border crossing into Benin is slightly easier than some of the other neighbouring countries, probably because so many people use it, unlike some of the less-frequented borders. The documents you might require and need to carry are:

a. International Certificate for Motor Vehicles which can be obtained from Police HQ, Moloney Street, Lagos.

b. Brown card for 3rd party insurance in West Africa. This is obtained from your Nigerian Insurance Company.

c. Visas for each person in the vehicle, which can be obtained from the Embassy of the Benin Republic, Victoria Island, Lagos.

d. Driving licence for Nigeria. If you have an International Driving Licence Permit 1920 or 1949 or both, take them.

e. Vaccination certificate for yellow fever. This is not normally asked for, but take it just in case.

f. West African CFA for hotels, etc. Take some small change for tolls and dash.

g. *A laissez - passer* is obtained at the borders of Benin Republic (and also Togo) at a cost of CFA 2,000.

Other tourist sites

There are a number of interesting places in both south and north Benin. In the Cotonou area there are:

a. *Ganvie.* Ganvie is a village built on stilts above the water and is called the tropical Venice. It is about 18 km north of Cotonou. To reach it, follow the Lome road (Togo) for about 10 km to a fork/roundabout then go right for 8 km past the Benin University to a petrol station on the right. Turn right to the car park and the office is 300 m down the road. The cost of the trip is approx CFA 4,000 each by motor canoe and it includes a drink at Ganvie. There is a gift shop where you are obliged to purchase! Take some coins for dashing children for photographs, etc. There is a restaurant, *La Pirogue,* close to the wharf.

b. *Ouidah.* Ouidah is just off the Lome (Togo) road close to the Togo border. It was a Portuguese enclave until 1961 and has a fort, Sao Joan Balista. There is a small museum in the old governor's villa. Ouidah is known for the infamous slave trade conducted from its port. Many thousands of slaves were shipped from the town. It is also the centre of a voodoo cult and has a voodoo 'temple' dedicated to the sacred python. The 'temple' is opposite the cathedral - an odd juxtaposition! Several live pythons are kept in the 'temple'.

Ouidah has an interesting history, having been captured in 1727 by the female 'Amazons' of King Agadja of Abomey, so it is worth exploring. Just a few kilometres north-west of Ouidah lies Lake Aheme. On the western shore is Issotome which has a mineral-water spring and women come from kilometres around to collect the water.

c. *Abomey.* Abomey, 135 km north of Cotonou, was the capital of the powerful kingdom of the Dan-Home. Behind the high walls of the Royal Palace stands a most significant historical museum. The walls are well worth seeing for the reliefs depicting the various kings. Abomey was founded in 1658 and had a powerful army of 'Amazons' under King Gbeharisin who ruled from 1889 to 1894. Abomey is well-known for its handicrafts connected with royalty, and for its bronzes. Like Ouidah, the city is also known for its voodoo.

d. *Parakou.* Parakou is on the north-south route which runs from the border with Niger to the coast. The *Hotel des Routiers* is beautiful and secluded, and is an excellent stopping point on the route. It has excellent food and a swimming pool.

e. *Northern Benin.* Few get to northern Benin, but if you can find the time, you may see people of the Somba tribe who, of the many tribes in Benin, have preserved their customs. They are renowned for their 'Tatas', unique 2-storey clay buildings with defensive towers. The north has 2 game reserves: *Pendjari*

National Park and the *'W' National Park.* Pendjari is wilder than most parks and few visitors go there. It is advisable not to go there alone. It is close to the Atakora mountain range which has spectacular scenery. The countryside around Natitingou is attractive hill country with waterfalls, and there is a particularly spectacular drive from Natitingou due west to Naboulgou.

f. *Porto-Novo.* Porto-Novo is the capital of Benin and there are obvious signs of its colonial past. There is a small Folk Museum with weapons, tools, domestic utensils and royal insignia. About 8 km from Porto Novo is Adjarra where they make drums of many sizes, colours and materials.

When in Benin, use the Sheraton Hotel as a base, but do not neglect the area thereabout. One can find a good hotel with a swimming pool in many places, but can you see a Ganvie, an Abomey or a Ouidah? The answer surely, is 'No'!

CAMEROON

Travel documents
The following travelling documents are required at the border:

a. Passport with Cameroonian visa from Cameroon Embassy, Lagos, or the Cameroon Counsul in Calabar.

b. Vaccination certificate (yellow fever).

c. Car documents (registration card, driving licence for Nigeria, international driving licence if you have one).

d. International Certificate for Motor Vehicles from the Lagos Police HQ, Moloney Street, Lagos. May not be necessary, but worth having just in case.

e. Insurance. Third party insurance can only be obtained in Cameroon. Few seem to be able to find a place to issue them. Obtain comprehensive insurance from your own insurer.

f. A letter of free passage, if you have an important Cameroonian friend who can provide one.

g. Currency. Central African CFA. Some travellers said they have been able to use West African CFA, but others like us found West African CFA useless. Travellers' cheques may be worth carrying as a reserve. Naira is not a good currency in Cameroon, though sterling and US dollars are. American Express credit cards are accepted in some hotels.

h. Nigerian Customs Re-importation Certificate, issued at the border by the customs. This is necessary for your return journey, so insist on it.

Petrol

Petrol in Cameroon is over £2 a gallon, much more expensive than in Nigeria. Sometimes, it is difficult to obtain. So fill up your tank well before the border and and carry at least one can. Do not rely upon filling up at the border as they may have run out.

Waza National Park

General

Waza National Park (Parc National de Waza) is in north Cameroon. It is said to be one of the best game reserves in West Africa. It is in the very north of Cameroon parallel with Bama, south-east of Maiduguri, in Nigeria. It is 205 km from Maiduguri and is best visited in the dry season, between November and June. It is recommended that you visit near the end of the dry season when the grass has died down and you can see the animals more clearly. It is partly wooded and partly savanna grassland. It has an area of 170,000 hectares and there are several roads running through it, unlike Yankari or Borgu Game Reserves which are not traversed by normal traffic. The variety of animals is greater than at Yankari. For example, there are giraffe, lion, hippotamus, elephant, antelope, cob, buffalo and many birds. Ostrich and Zebra have been imported into the reserve, so there is much to see. There are two 'campements' overlooking the best waterholes. It is believed that the main hotel has just been refurbished. All reports say it is well worth a visit, but allow 3 days to get there from Lagos, unless you fly to Maiduguri.

Other tourist sites

You may wish to do a little touring further south. Be prepared for some very poor roads and avoid the wet season. Some places to visit are:

Maroua. It is an unspoilt market town. Hotels, Muzao or Le Sare.

Rhumsiki. This place has a spectacular scenery. Campement Rhumsiki is a good hotel.

Garoua. Garoua is a large town which has a supermarket. The Novotel de la Bepone is an impressive hotel.

Ngaoundere. This is a town on a 914 m plateau. Ranch de Ngaoundaba is 40 km from the town. Go out on the Meiganga road (N1); pass through Wakwa and Dibi and on your right (west) is the Ranch Hotel. A double room costs CFA 11,000 (£21) approximately as at 1989. This first-class hotel is run by a Frenchwoman, and is well worth a visit.

Unless you have to, do not travel south of the Ranch de Ngaoundere, because the roads are terrible. Leave the south of Cameroon to another visit, and approach from Ikom.

Route

The following route is recommended. From Lagos, a first night stop at Abuja is advised, with either Bauchi or Yola as the suggested second night's stop. On the third day, drive to Bama and from there to the border, then to Mora and north-east to Waza. In Waza, ask for the Parc National. Do not try to get there in 2 days as the border crossing could take some time. It is best to use the Bama crossing as other border roads are not in good condition.

Hotels

The National Park has its own hotel, *Hoteliere du Camppement,* with 100 beds. The food is said to be excellent and the rondavels clean and well-maintained. Today's cost is not known, but assume that it is between CFA 16,000 and CFA 20,000 (£32 to £40) with lunch and dinner costing about CFA 5,000 each per person. American Express cards are accepted, but no others. The cost of entering the National park is approxiately CFA 1,500 per person (£3).

Bamenda

General

Bamenda (in the south of Cameroon) is in the highlands. The surrounding area is very scenic indeed and the drive from Nigeria starts through the thick rainforest of the unique Korup Reserve. From Mamfe onwards the road climbs through the most beautiful mountain scenery to Bali and to the high grassland plateau of Bamenda. Though the town of Bamenda is not of special interest, the countryside is magnificent and is a great change from the steamy humidity of Lagos. The cool, clear air and lovely tropical evenings are quite a pleasure, especially sitting out in the garden of the *Skyline Hotel,* which is above the town on the edge of an escarpment. A few kilometres from Bamenda is Bafut, the home of the Fon of Bafut, whose father was immortalised by Gerald Durrell in his books, *The Bafut Beagles* and *A Zoo in my Luggage.* In Bamenda, there is an interesting craft centre which you pass on the way to the Skyline Hotel, but prices are expensive compared with Nigeria.

Facing the future together

Thirty years ago, Nigeria's oil production was just beginning. Gradually, the nation's natural resources have been unlocked, led by Shell's pioneering technical innovation. Today, Nigeria is a world-scale oil exporter, committed to boosting reserves and production. Within reach is a bold new Shell-led export initiative: liquefied natural gas.

Nigeria's other great resource is its people. Shell is balancing its economic and technical contributions with a growing range of community programmes – education, agriculture and the environment. As the country's pioneering and leading oil company, Shell is helping to build a brighter future for all Nigerians.

The Shell Petroleum Development Company of Nigeria Ltd
Operator of the NNPC/Shell Joint Venture

WAPCO products depict STRENGTH and BEAUTY

and now... Electrical Motor Repair Services

PORTLAND CEMENT – For over 20 years, the West African Portland Cement Company Limited has been producing the Elephant Portland Cement which meets the highest international standards for ordinary Portland Cement. About 1½ million tonnes of *Elephant Portland Cement* are now produced annually and are used in the widest variety of new building projects which are vital to Nigeria's bright future: universities, bridges, offices, factories, buildings – big or small. *Elephant Portland Cement* has gone a long way in giving strength to the nation's construction efforts. It is the leader in the market.

PORTLAND PRODUCTS – The Portland Products Division offers a variety of special products for beautiful decorative finishes such as – Bluetex Roller Applied Texture Finish, Sandtex Decorating and Surface treatment. These products will enhance the appearance of any building and at the same time fight effectively against fungicide and other organic growths.

ELECTRICAL SERVICES – The Portland Electrical Repairs Division offers you reliable high quality servicing of your run-down motors. This new division repairs and rewinds various types of Electrical Machines, giving them a new lease of life. Though this division is still young, our already long list of reputable clients confirm our efficiency. Save valuable foreign exchange by using our services.

Our sign of quality shown here is affixed to all our works

WAPCO
THE WEST AFRICAN PORTLAND CEMENT COMPANY LIMITED
Head Office: Kilometre 12, Elephant House, Ikorodu Road, P. O. Box 1001 Lagos. Telephone 901060 – 3

THERMOCOOL
T300

We call it the T300
you will call it Beautiful . . .
– the reliable family
Refrigerator.

Make things better . . .
. . . Make better things

Other tourist sites

A visit to Bafut, north-west of Bamenda is definitely worthwhile, as the Fon's Palace is of interest, and vividly described by Gerald Durell in *The Bafut Beagles*. There is beautiful scenery towards Kumbo with extensive tea plantations, and an American Baptist Mission at Ndu to the north-east of Bamenda, but once again, the roads are laterite and travelling is slow.

Route

From Lagos, I recommend that you take 3 days to reach Bamenda as the roads vary from good, bad to indifferent. From Lagos to Enugu the road is good, but the route from Enugu to Ikom via Abakaliki was very bad in 1990. The alternative is via Onitsha - Aba - Ikot Ekpene - Ikom. There is a motel called the Metro at Ikom which is adequate, (see 'Alok' on page 47). Ikom is close to the border at Ekok. From the border, it is laterite all the way to Bamenda and it took us about 6 hours after at least an hour at the border. The route is then via Mamfe - Bali - Bamenda. Sometimes the road is very narrow, especially the bridges, and extremely winding and steep in the mountain area. A 4-wheel drive vehicle is recommended, especially a Range Rover which has superb suspension. Do not travel in the wet season as the roads may be dangerous and you may be in clouds most of the time.

Hotels

The best hotel is the *Skyline Hotel* which has a Belgian proprietor. As mentioned earlier, it is at the top of the escarpment overlooking the town of Bamenda and has wonderful views especially at sunset and in the early mornings. There is a swimming-pool, which felt decidedly chilly after Lagos swimming-pools, but was very refreshing. If for any reason you are delayed on the journey, the small *Inland Hotel* at Mamfe could be a possible overnight stop en route, as it is never advisable to drive in West Africa after dark, and especially not on this route.

Limbe (Victoria)

General

The old town of Victoria has now been renamed Limbe and is on the sea, west of Douala. It shows evidence of its varied colonial past - German, British and French. Fortunately, most people in this area speak English. Limbe nestles under the formidable Mount Cameroon which, at 4,095 m, is the highest mountain in West Africa. It is an active volcano but unfortunately it is often covered in cloud. On a clear day the off-shore island of Bioko (formerly Fernando Po), can also be seen. 'Victoria' was the capital of British Cameroon and a legacy of those days can still be seen in the architecture of the houses. The area around the town is scenic and pleasant, and there is an interesting botanical garden. Limbe is worth a visit and is infinitely preferable to either Douala or Yaounde for the tourist. Like most places in West Africa, it is better to see it in the dry season when there is little cloud to obscure the views - unless there is harmattan instead! The worst months for harmattan are December and January, but it can last into February.

Tourist sites

A visit to Buea just below Mount Cameroon is well worthwhile. There is a hotel called the *Mountain Hotel* in Buea. It is quite reasonable, clean and has a basic restaurant. Buea is an old German town and has many signs of its past history with a castle (Schloss), and houses with German architecture. It is about 24 km from Victoria. Buea is the starting point for any climb of Mount Cameroon, but ask for a guide before ascending. If you have more time for exploration, ask in Limbe because there is a coast road around the south of Mount Cameroon to Idenao, which is 41 km from Limbe. In the other direction is the Bimbia River and Mabeta, (18 km), which may bring an interesting change of scenery.

Route

Please see Bamenda page 124 for the route to Mamfe in Cameroon. Instead of continuing straight on to Bamenda, turn right (south) at Bachuo Akakbe, 17 km past Mamfe, onto the N8. Pass through Nguti to Kumba and thence to Limbe (Victoria). Only the latter part of the route from Kumba is tarred.

Hotels

There are 2 hotels in Victoria: the *Atlantic Beach Hotel* and the *Miramar*. The former is on the coast on a rock promontory and is graded 'very good'. It has an excellent open-air terraced restaurant and a lovely view on the seaward side. You pay extra for a sea view, but it is worth it. The food is excellent, especially the seafood. The hotel is not very expensive. 1989 prices were CFA 15,900 (£30) a night. A typical 2-day stay, indulging in plenty of good food and drink, might cost about £100 ($180 or DM300). It is recommended that you take Central African CFA, (see page 122 on currency).

Recommended further reading

Nigel Barley's *The Innocent Anthropologist* and *A Plague of Caterpillars* are about northern Cameroon and are extremely entertaining.

MALI

Timbuktu (Timbouctou via Niamey)

General

Timbuktu has a strange fascination. The name has almost become part of the English language, signifying 'to travel to the back of beyond'. It has distant memories of great explorers like

Mungo Park and is mentioned in most history books on the exploration of Africa. Nowadays, however, apart from its romance, there is not a great deal to see. Those who have been there, however, declare that it was worth it as an unforgettable experience, and of course, now they can always drop the conversation-stopping words, 'When I was in Timbuktu' at a cocktail party and be sure of an awed reaction. The town itself is close to the Niger River. In fact, for most of the journey the route lies along that great river. The important point about this trip is that sound planning is essential and you should always have at least 2 vehicles in the party.

Route

There are 2 possible routes from Lagos. The more conventional one is Lagos - Sokoto - Illela (Nigerian border) - Birni n'Koni (border) - Niamey - Tillabery - Ayorou - Labbazarga (Mali border)- Gao - Bourem - Timbuktu, much of the way following the course of the Niger River. The route to Tillabery is tarred. But from there it gets progressively worse as it is laterite to Labbazarga and then the road becomes ill-defined, badly corrugated or soft-sand piste. This part of the journey is for 4-wheel drive vehicles only and sand ladders and shovels are advisable. The total journey from Lagos to Timbuktu and return is approximately 6,000 km.

The alternative route is to go through the Benin Republic from Lagos - Cotonou - Parakou - Niamey - Tillabery - Gao - Bourem - Timbuktu. Either way, it is recommended that you take 6 days to get there and spend perhaps 2 days there. You would therefore need to allow at least 14 days for the trip.

Hotels

The recommended hotels en route are as follows: Sokoto *(Giginya)* - Niamey *(Grand* or *Terminus* but if you want to spend a lot of money, *Le Gawaye Hotel)* - Gao *(Atlantide* or the motel near the airport outside the town) - or why not stop at the *Hotel Amenokal* at Ayorou on the River Niger about 200 km north of

Niamey - Timbuktu (*Azalai* or the *Sofitel*, but according to our informant, you need a 4-wheel drive vehicle to get to the front door of the latter which is a 5-star hotel!).

Travel documents

Visas are not required for the British in Niger, but they are for Mali. These may be obtained through the Mali Embassy in Accra. There is no embassy for Mali closer than Ghana, unfortunately. They can also be obtained through the Mali Embassy in Dakar, Senegal. Other nationalities should check their visa regulations with their own embassies or high commissions.

Other documents required are:

a. Yellow fever innoculation certificate.
b. Driving licence (Nigerian will do).
c. Car registration book.
d. Insurance certificate extended to Niger and Mali.
e. International certificate for motor vehicles.

Ensure that your passport is stamped at both borders to prove that you have crossed legally. Also ensure that you obtain a *laissez-passer*, again at both borders, which must be surrendered on leaving the country.

Police posts are definitely delaying factors in Niger and Mali. Remember to check into the police station at all towns where you spend the night.

Petrol

Petrol in Nigeria is normally plentiful, but there are occasional shortages, especially at Christmas time. It is important to fill up in Sokoto. Petrol from there on is less reliable, but there should be petrol at Niamey, Dessa and Gao. You need to plan on no petrol from Gao onwards; so carry cans to cover 1,000 km without petrol. There may be petrol in Timbuktu itself, but you cannot rely on this.

Niamey

If you wish to go no further than Niamey, you will not be too disappointed. The 'Game Parc du W' is 150 km south of the town, close to the Benin border, and is reputed to be as good as Yankari. Niamey has good shopping, a museum and zoo, and at Boubon 20 km from Niamey on the Tillabery road, you can buy interesting pottery at very reasonable prices.

A good guide book is *The Sahara Handbook* by Roger Lascelles.

NIGER

Zinder

General

Zinder is close to the Nigeria/Niger border, but it is quite different from Nigerian towns, even those close to the border, because of its Saharan/French character. It is relatively easy to get to Zinder from Kano. Zinder is an attractive town with a large open-air market, 2 expensive supermarkets and a couple of hotels. The Zinder Club has a pool and bar and is not too expensive. The Mirimah market is at an oasis 30 km from Zinder and is held on Sundays. It is a very colourful scene as finely dressed Touaregs form the majority of the local population, and the market has some interesting things for sale, including camels. Zinder has a typical 'Beau Geste' fort on top of a hill, which is still used as a military fort, so it is best not photographed. The ability to speak even a little French will help a lot.

Route

The recommended route is Lagos - Kaduna - Kano - Daura - then north to the border and on to Zinder.

Hotels

There are 3 hotels, the *Damagaran* which is rather rundown, the *Central* and the *Amadou Koura Daga* on the Niamey road. (It is on the left as you enter Zinder from the west). This latter hotel has recently been visited and personally recommended as it has better food, is cheaper and the car can be parked inside a protected compound. Hotels are not expensive in Niger but they will expect you to pay in West African CFA. The price is approximately £20 a night for a room.

Travel documents

Visas are not required for British nationals visiting Niger, but other nationalities should check the visa regulations with their own embassy or high commission.

Other documents required are:

a. Yellow fever innoculation certificate.
b. Driving licence (Nigerian will do).
c. Car registration book.
d. Insurance certificate extended to Niger.
e. International certificate for motor mehicles.

Please ensure that your passport is stamped at the border to prove that you have crossed legally and also that you obtain a *laissez-passer* which must be surrendered at the border again when you leave the country.

Agadez

General

Agadez is a mediaeval trading centre at the southern edge of the Sahara, an entrepot for the 'Azelai' camel trains emanating from Bilma. It is on the main route across the Sahara to Tamanrasset in Algeria. The sights to see are the mosque, the market, which is typically Touareg, and a smaller Hausa market in the centre of the town where craft-work, Touareg jewellery, silver and antiques are sold. It helps if you speak French or Hausa. You never really encounter the real desert, but you are not far from it.

If you should have travellers' cheques, it is necessary to have a photocopy of the original receipt before you can change them. This is because there is often no operational photocopier available.

Other tourist sites

a. About 120 km south-west of Agadez is *In Gall*, a pleasant small oasis with a 'Beau Geste' fort. In Gall is off the main Agadez - Tahoua road and is a 100 km diversion.

b. Tafadek, 50 km north of Agadez has some thermal springs which are said to be worth a visit. Further tours can be organised from Agadez if you ask at your hotel.

Route

The recommended route is Lagos - Kaduna - Sokoto - Birni Nkoni (Niger border) - Tahoua - Agadez. The distance from Lagos is approximately 2,000 km. It is suggested that you take 3 days over the journey with possible stops at Abuja and Sokoto. The roads from Lagos to Agadez are tarred all the way. It is advisable to take petrol cans because petrol in Niger is expensive and not as plentiful as in Nigeria. The round trip is at least 7 or 8 days journey. Do ensure that your *laissez-passer* includes all the places you wish to visit. Report to the police when you arrive at Agadez.

Hotels

There are only 2 reasonable hotels in Agadez, the *Hotel de l'Air* and the *Telwa*. The Hotel de l'Air is recommended; it is simple but good. Plan on about £20 a night with meals and extra. Payment is made in CFA.

Travel documents

See, Zinder page 130.

TOGO

Lome

General

Lome, the capital of Togo, is a well-laid out, clean and attractive seaside city, showing a strong French influence. The hotels are of a high standard, as are the many restaurants, and parts of the town are reminiscent of the south of France. The drive to Lome, apart from the border crossings, is easy and the road is in good condition all the way. Some stretches are close to the palm-fringed coast and it makes a pleasant break in the drive to have a walk along the deserted beach. Lome superficially resembles the south of France with wide streets, well-built colonial mansions, traffic lights that work and an impression of calmness and order. It takes between 6 and 8 hours from Lagos by car, depending on the borders and your determination to drive there without delay. Sea-bathing in Togo is just as dangerous as in Nigeria or Benin, so take great care. All the big hotels have good pools, so it is not necessary to swim in the sea. Togo was a German colony until after the First World War when it became French, but it gained its independence on 27th April 1960. It is served by an international airport so it is possible to fly from Lagos. For golfers, there is a golf course near Lome. Ask for directions from your hotel.

Tourist sites

a. *Lake Togo.* Lake Togo is on the route, 28 km east of Lome. The Hotel du Lac is very peaceful and less expensive than in Lome. A canoe trip across the shallow lake to Togoville, where there is an old mission, is not expensive and is a pleasant outing.

b. *Kpalime* (pronounced Palime). This is a historic town about 122 km from Lome. The south-west of Togo is mountainous and has lovely scenic drives. A journey to Kpalime climbs up the Avalime massif leading to Mt Agou over 900 m high and to Viale Castle, a mediaeval style building with wonderful views of the surrounding contryside. Unfortunately, the road up Mt Agou is now said to be impassable. Near Mt Agou (30 km south of Kpalime and 85 km from Lome) is the Bethania, a very pleasant dairy-farm hotel with nice rooms and a small swimming pool, which is personally recommended. Also en route is Assahoun, with handicrafts for sale. There is a hotel in Kpalime called the Grand Hotel du 30 Aout.

c. *Kove Wildlife Park/Forest of Fazoo.* The park is approximately 3 hours drive from Lome.

Route

The route is via Cotonou in the Benin Republic (see page 118). The road forks as you leave Cotonou. It is possible to make a mistake but the correct route is marked to Lome. However, if in doubt, ask. The road is parallel to the coast most of the way. Petrol is expensive in Togo, so fill up in Nigeria before you cross to Benin.

Hotels

The international hotels are the *Hotel Sarakawa, Hotel de la Paix, the Hotel du 2 Fevrier* and the *Hotel Tropicana.* I would recommend the Sarakawa which is on the beach. It gives a discount to diplomats and credit cards may be used if you wish, otherwise the currency is West African CFA. Costs are fairly high in comparison with Nigeria, as they are between £40 and £50 a room with main meals costing about £20 a head. There are many restaurants in the town to suit a variety of purses.

Travel documents

(See page 118 on Benin).

7

Countries on A Direct Flight from Nigeria

EGYPT

KENYA

ZIMBABWE

BRAZIL

GREAT BRITAIN

General Introduction

This chapter is designed for the international traveller who has the opportunity of breaking his journey on a flight from Lagos back to Europe, or who can take advantage of a direct flight to see the wonderful game parks of Kenya or Zimbabwe, for example. Why fly straight back to Europe when you have the chance of dropping in to Cairo, or even Rio perhaps?

EGYPT

Cairo
General

Egypt is the cradle of civilisation, and visiting the historical sites in Egypt, one can imagine how people lived many, many centuries ago. There is so much to see that the ideal would be a 2-week holiday exploring Cairo, cruising up the River Nile to Luxor, Aswan and Abu Simbel, and perhaps visiting Alexandria, Sharm El Sheikh, Mt Sinai and Hurghada. If you have only a few days, it is best to stay in Cairo - you can feast yourself on its many wonderful sights, including the fascinating Egyptian Museum (with its exhibits from the tomb of Tutankamen), the pyramids of Giza, the Sphinx, palaces, mosques, forts, the Citadel, the Nile and many night activities, including the 'Son et Lumiere' at Giza.

The markets, especially the Khan El Kalili bazaar, are worth a visit just to see the huge variety of goods for sale. The Egyptian salesman is a masterful trader, and all your bargaining skills will be needed to outwit him! The nightlife is variable, exciting and tempting, but above all Cairo is a cultural centre. The hotels are excellent, (and are not as expensive as first-class hotels), and the service is good. The Egyptians love visitors and look after them very well indeed, so much so that they have tourist police to see that visitors are protected from cheats and fraudsters and most tourist guides are graduates in tourism. There are many reliable tourist agents who can organise trips for you once you get to Cairo. Egypt should be a place that everyone visits en route from Nigeria to Europe as it is a truly fascinating city, and provides an immense contrast to both places.

Itinerary

It is not easy to give an itinerary for Cairo and Egypt except to give you some idea of what to see and how long you should stay in each place.

a. Cairo - not less than 3 full days and 1 day on your return journey.
b. Luxor - 3 days You can do a 5-day (4-night) boat trip up the Nile or go by overnight train which is less expensive, but good value.

c. Aswan - 2 days
d. Abu Simbel - 1 day
e. Alexandria or El Arish - 2 days
f. Sinai - 1-3 days (Dahab and Taba on the Gulf of Aquaba).
g. Sharm El Sheikh - 1-2 days or more if you are a keen skin-diver.

During a 2-week holiday, you will need to allow at least 2 days for travel up the Nile, or you can travel by air.

Travel documents

You do need a visa for Egypt, which can be obtained from the Egyptian Embassy, 182 B Kofo Abayomi Street, Victoria Island. The normal travel documents, i.e. passport, vaccination certificate are also needed. It is no longer necessary to change the equivalent of £100 at the airport, as this regulation has been cancelled. Currency must be changed officially in a 'Bureau de Change' or bank. The black market is definitely discouraged. Customs and Excise will almost certainly check to see that you have converted your currency officially, so keep your receipts carefully.

Route

Egypt Air fly from Lagos to Cairo on Mondays and Thursdays returning on Wednesdays and Sundays. Normally all aircraft stop at Kano en route. There are plenty of internal flights within Egypt and, of course, international flights to Europe, the Middle East, Far East and the USA. Flying Egypt Air via Cairo is recognisd as one of the cheapest ways of travelling to Europe. It is recommended that you travel first class, which is excellent. The Egypt Air Office is at 39/41 Martins Street, off Broad Street in Lagos. Tel: 661102, 661974.

Cost

Some diplomatic missions have agreements with hotels in Cairo where you can get a discount. Normally, a hotel will cost you about £30 to £40 a night, depending on the grade of the hotel. An Egyptian pound is worth about a quarter of one pound sterling at today's rate.

Hotels

Cairo is full of excellent hotels. All the big hotel groups like the *Sheraton* and *Hilton* have a hotel there. We stayed in *Shepheard's Hotel* which is on the River Nile in a central position and is very pleasant. *Marriott's* is also recommended as one of the best.

Time of year to visit

We went to Cairo in July/August, which is the hottest season, but one advantage was that tourist sites were not overcrowded. The season is all the year round, with the high season being December to February.

KENYA

Nairobi

General

Kenya is known to be one of the most highly-developed tourist countries in the world and certainly in Africa. The fame of its wildlife, and the scenery with its great Rift Valley lakes, snow-capped Mt Kenya and fabulous beaches, is almost unequalled in Africa. Few people have not heard of 'Tree Tops' or 'The Ark', the game-viewing lodges which are both in the Aberdare Mountains. The pink flamingoes on Lake Nakuru are seldom matched as a spectacle even for those not particularly interested in birds. One could go on and on extolling the assets of Kenya, but apart from its scenery, Kenya has a very pleasant climate owing to its height above sea level. A further advantage is that it welcomes tourists with open arms, mostly because the economy depends upon foreign currency earned through tourism. Both Ethiopian Airlines and Nigerian Airways fly to Nairobi, and the former has a particularly good reputation. The booking office for Ethiopian Airlines is in Tafawa Balewa Square. Ethiopian Airlines fly either via Kinshasa or Douala. Like most places I have selected, you will never regret a visit to Kenya, and it is an experience you will remember all your life. Many tourist agencies divide a 2-week holiday into one week on safari and one week on the beach at Malindi or one of the resorts near Mombasa.

It is possible to book safaris through a company called UTC (United Touring Company) in Nairobi which has been recommended by a friend in Lagos who booked through them. They are a London-based company but their address in Kenya is P O Box 42196, Nairobi, Kenya, and their 'Safaritrail bookings' telex number is 22228, or book through your own travel agent. Another personally recommended travel agent in Nairobi is Bunson Travel Service Ltd. Their address is Box 45456, Nairobi, Kenya, and their telex number is 22071. Please note that to hire a Landrover or similar vehicle for a private safari is very expensive, but for the adventurous there are even Camel and Horseback safaris.

Tourist sites

It is impossible to mention all the game reserves and beach resorts, so ask for advice from a travel agent, but some of the 'not to be missed' places are:

a. *Nairobi.* It is the capital of Kenya and the starting point for most of the safaris. The Nairobi National Park just outside the city is worth a visit as it has a variety of animals including lion and rhino, and is a pleasant day's outing. It also has an animal 'orphanage' where motherless animals are cared for.

b. *Maasai Mara Game Reserve.* This is probably the most famous reserve in Kenya and borders the Serengeti National Park in Tanzania. You can stay at either the Keekorok Lodge Hotel or the new Maasai Mara Sopa Lodge. Hot air balloon game-viewing trips can be organised from the Keekorok Lodge, but are very expensive. To see 25 species of game in a day is not unusual, so 2 full days at the Maasai Mara should be adequate. There are many other famous game reserves like Tsavo, Amboseli and Samburu, but each travel agent has its own 'package' of nights at game reserves for you to choose from, according to your own particular interests.

c. *Lake Nakuru.* Huge flocks of flamingoes are usually found at Lake Nakuru and they are an unforgettable sight, but check first that they are in residence, as sometimes they depart for other lakes. We also saw a wide variety of water-birds, including pelican, African spoonbill, plovers, avocets and yellow-billed storks. The Lake Nakuru Lodge Hotel was only 'satisfactory' when we stayed there in 1984. Lake Naivasha is another interesting Rift Valley lake with an excellent hotel, the Safari Lodge, closer to Nairobi.

d. *'Treetops' or 'The Ark'* in the Aberdare Mountains. These are 2 game viewing lodges in the reserve, and as they are in a montane habitat rather than the savannah of the Maasai Mara, they are well worth a visit both for the scenery and the climate. In the case of The Ark, visitors stay at the Aberdare Country Club and are then taken by bus to The Ark for dinner and a night's game-viewing from the balconies. There are bells in each bedroom so that you can be called if interesting animals come down to the illuminated waterhole after you have gone to bed. We saw elephant, buffalo, giant forest hog, hyena, bushbuck, to mention just a few, but the rare bongo did not make its appearance, unfortunately. If you stay at the Outspan Hotel, a similar arrangement is made to escort visit-

Lever Brothers Nigeria PLC
—making world-renowned brands a must in every home

When it comes to enhancing the quality of life of Nigerians with first class brands, the name that instantly comes to mind is Lever Brothers Nigeria PLC.

In nearly every Nigerian home, brands from the wide range of LBN products are used daily.

The ever growing number of successful brands the company makes, includes such internationally renowned names as Omo, Surf, Lux, Sunlight, Close-Up, Vaseline, Lipton, Blue Band, Tree Top among others.

Lever Brothers Nigeria PLC has been dedicated to the production of such top quality brands for Nigerians for over 60 years-time enough to earn the distinction of being the market leader.

LBN

Lever Brothers Nigeria PLC
A must in every home

Sales·Parts·Service Available at:

Allens

A DIVISION OF **JOHN HOLT** LIMITED

MERCEDES BENZ

VOLKSWAGEN

BRANCHES:- APAPA. BENIN. ENUGU. JOS. KADUNA. KANO. PORTHARCOURT. WARRI.

May & Baker
a trusted name for quality Pharmaceutical products, Industrial and Fine chemicals

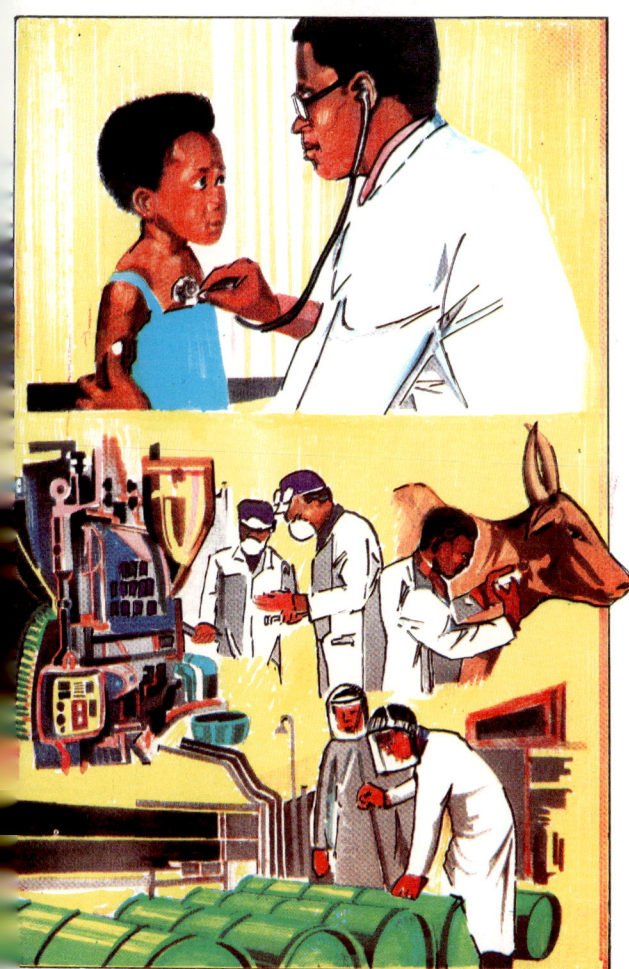

Established since 1944, May & Baker is one of the leading manufacturers of high quality family health care products like the popular Nivaquine range, Tixylix and other cough syrups, M&B 5 (branded paracetamol) as well as prescription products.

Other areas of activities include the marketing of a wide range of animal health products, Laboratory, bulk pharmaceutical and other chemicals for many local industrial needs.

May and Baker is also fully geared to developing and diversifying its business into other related areas of local manufacture and contributes to the development of research and pharmaceutical training in the country.

M & B   **MAY & BAKER**
The nations first name in chemicals & pharmaceuticals

HEAD OFFICE:
May & Baker Nigeria PLC
3/5 Sapara Street
Industrial Estate
P.M.B. 21049, Ikeja
Lagos
Phone: 900200 – 5

Telex: 26258 MANDB NIG

SPECTRUM ROAD MAP OF NIGERIA

In an expanding country like Nigeria, where growth is constant, it is vital to have the most up-to-date maps available. The new Spectrum Road Map of Nigeria is fully revised, clear and comprehensive. International and state boundaries, expressways, roads and tracks are included, along with all communications i.e. railways, major and minor airports, rivers and ferries. There is useful information on local landscape types -swamps and areas likely to flood. Full contour colouring allows the lie of the land to be judged at a glance. For short journeys or long treks - the Spectrum Road Map of Nigeria is an invaluable companion.

Size: 762 × 1016mm (30" × 40") Flat
255 × 140mm (10" × 5½") Folded
Scale: 1:1 500 000

Available from airports and leading bookshops, or in case of difficulty from:
Spectrum Books Ltd, Sunshine House,
Second Commercial Road, Oluyole Estate,
Ibadan, PMB 5612.
Telex: 31588   Telephone 310058-311215

ors to 'Treetops' for overnight game-viewing. Game-viewing trips can also be arranged in the park, and there are an excellent variety of birds, including the huge crowned eagle, for the the keen bird-watcher.

e. *Lake Baringo.* This is to the north of the country, in the Rift Valley and has a good hotel, *The Lake Baringo Hotel,* beside the lake. This area is particularly interesting for its birds and there is a resident ornithologist who takes visitors on bird-walks along the edge of the escarpment, beside the lake, or on a boat trip. There are also many hippos to be seen in the lake.

f. *Mombasa and Malindi.* These are two most popular tourist places on the coast, but there are beaches and excellent hotels all along the coast. It is possible to take a night train trip from Nairobi to Mombasa. Malindi is about 100 km north of Mombasa and has a marine reserve where it is possible to snorkel in safety. Malindi is also excellent for watersports and big-game fising.

Time of year to visit

The rainy season is between March and June, with the 'small rains' in November, and these months should be avoided. The high season is around Christmas and the New Year.

Travel documents

Kenya does not require British visitors to have a visa, but other nationals should check with their embassy or the Kenyan High Commission at Oyinkan Abayomi Drive, Ikoyi, to make sure. Tel: 682768 or 685531. Both yellow-fever and cholera certificates are required.

Travellers' cheques or any hard currency can be exchanged for Kenyan shillings which are approximately 30 to one pound sterling, but as exchange rates vary so much, this must be checked when you are planning your trip.

Hotels

There are numerous high-grade hotels in Kenya, so get your travel agent to find one to suit your pocket. The *Norfolk Hotel* is one of the most renowned in Nairobi, or you may prefer the *Nairobi Hilton,* or the *Intercontinental* to name just a few. Hotels in the game parks are usually excellent. Costs are difficult to estimate, but a 10-14 day holiday will cost over £1,000 per person. Do not forget that in the highlands of Kenya, it gets quite cool at night and some warm clothing may be required.

ZIMBABWE

Harare

General

Zimbabwe has a highly-organised and efficient tourist industry like Kenya. Its hotels are first-rate and the staff are of the highest quality. This, on top of the superb tourist sites that Zimbabwe has to offer, must make it a favourite for those who like to travel in Africa. The tourist guides label it as having 'everything under the sun'. It is a country rich in history and culture, whose stunning scenery and varied geography are a delight. The country can be divided into 3 main areas of interest:

a. Harare and its surrounding area.
b. Victoria Falls, Lake Kariba, Hwange National Park, Matusadona National Park.
c. Eastern Highlands.

Zimbabwe has a pleasant climate, especially in the winter months, (European summer), as much of it is well above sea level, and it is cool at night. The dry season is September and October which can be hot for those not used to the heat. The rainy season is November to March, the Zimbabwean summer, as of course, Zimbabwe is south of the equator. Some warm clothing may be needed at night, except in the lower areas like Victoria Falls and Kariba.

Itinerary

It is always difficult to recommend an itinerary, because every individual has a different view of what constitutes a good holiday. Some like to go to one place and relax, others like to dash around seeing as much as they can. A recommended schedule might be:

a. Harare, Ewanrigg Botanical Gardens, Hanging Rocks Game Park and other tourist sites close to the capital - 2 days and another day on the return journey.

b. Eastern Highlands - the Vumba Mountains and the White Horse Inn, Nyanga Mountains with its luxurious Troutbeck Inn, and Connemara Lakes, 3 to 4 days. At Troutbeck you can play golf, ride, fish and go boating, all with hired equipment. There is also a swimming pool.

c. Victoria Falls (2 days), Hwangi National Park (2 days), Lake Kariba (1 day), Bumi Hills (2 days) or Mana Pools National Park (2 days), total 7 days.

Travel documents

Visas are not required by visitors from most European countries, but check with the High Commission for Zimbabwe at 6 Kasumu Ekemode Street (off Saka Tinubu Street), Victoria Island, just in case. Tel: 619328. You will need a yellow fever certificate and also a cholera certificate if coming from a cholera area, so, it would be advisable to check before travelling. You are allowed to bring in any amount of hard currency, but this should be declared on arrival on a currency declaration form. It should be kept carefully throughout your stay. You should not bring in more than Z$20 in currency. Travellers cheques and credit cards are accepted in the main hotels, but in safari lodges credit cards may not be accepted. You should not leave the country with more than Z$20, and this needs to be carefully attended to.

Hotels

The hotels in Zimbabwe are well up to international tourist standards. The best hotels in Harare are *Meikles Hotel* and the very modern *Monomatapa Hotel* in the town, and the *Sheraton*, about 2 km outside. There are excellent hotels at tourist sites, which can be booked through your tourist agent. In Zimbabwe, the game drives are organised by the individual lodges, which you book on arrival.

Costs

Hotels vary but you will find the Harare ones will cost you between £50 and £80 a night (1990 prices). Outside Harare the hotels will be a little cheaper at £40 to £70 a night. Non-residents must be prepared to pay hotel bills and most other tourist costs in hard currency, for example, departure airport tax is £6.

Health

Like most African countries, swimming should be confined to hotel swimming pools because of the risk of bilharzia, and a malaria prophylactic should be taken.

Airlines

Balkan Airlines fly direct to Harare from Lagos. At present their schedule is to leave Lagos on Sundays, at 8.30 am and arriving at 3.00 pm local time. The flight returns on a Sunday, leaving Harare at 5.00 pm and arriving in Lagos at 9.00 pm local time. Travelling within the country is by Zimbabwe Airlines. Ghana Airlines have just inaugurated a direct flight to Harare, but as yet it is untried. The only other way is to fly Ethiopian Airlines via Addis Ababa and Nairobi, but it is a long way round!

Both Balkan and Ethiopian Airlines have offices in Tafawa Balewa Square. The safaris should be booked through your own travel agent.

BRAZIL
Rio

General

Brazil has been included because it is possible to fly direct from Lagos to Rio by Varig, the Brazilian Airline. The Airline arranges a special 'package tour' which consists of 6 nights in Rio, the fun capital of Brazil, with flights to and from Lagos, a first-class hotel and optional tours of the surrounding area, all at a very reasonable cost. There is also a 6-night Rio/Sao Paulo Business Package which includes one night in Rio before travelling on to Sao Paulo. Another tour includes 2 nights in Rio, 2 in Salvador, 1 in Foz do Iguachu (the fantastic waterfall featured in the film *The Mission),* and back to Rio. Note that there is a surcharge of $150 for a single person for these package deals.

Brazil, and especially Rio, is a place well worth visiting for the spectacular scenery, the nightlife, shopping, (especially for gemstones), the food and the fabulous beaches which are some of the best in the world. It is locally said that 'God created the world in 6 days and the 7th he devoted to Rio!' The world's greatest carnival is held in Rio in February, with wild, intoxicating days culminating in the great parade, Escola de Samba, but check with the airline for the exact dates if you wish to participate!

Itinerary

Your programme for the Rio trip will look something like this:

a. Monday, leave Lagos at 11.30 am and arrive Rio at 2.45 pm (local time). You will be met by an English-speaking guide and taken to the hotel you have selected. Bed and breakfast are included in the price, but lunch and dinner are extra.

b. Tuesday, city tour at 2.30 pm which will include Copacabana beach where, in the summer you will see some of the most beautiful girls in the world!

c. Wednesday, a free day for shopping with an optional tour to Plataforma I, where you can watch the attractive mulatas of Brazil dancing the Samba in their exotic dresses.

d. Thursday, free day for shopping guided to the Barrashopping if you feel inclined, or why not hire a car and tour outside Rio? A 'must' is the Sugar Loaf mountain. Take a cable car to the top where there are restaurants, shops and other entertainments, and of course, a fabulous view of Rio.

e. Friday, free day for shopping or an optional tour in a beautiful boat to the exotic tropical islands along Sepetiba Bay.

f. Saturday, free day for shopping or the beach, or take a trip to Petropolis, the Imperial City, with a chance to buy textiles at bargain prices. You can visit the Imperial Museum as well.

g. Sunday, last minute sight-seeing, with a trip to the famous statue 'Christ the Redeemer' with its breath-taking view of the city. The return flight to Lagos, Varig RG794, leaves Rio at 7.00 pm.

The above itinerary is only a guideline. Why not hop on a plane and see Salvador, Iguacu or Manaus on the Amazon River? Varig will advise you of the possibilities. Remember that Brazil is south of the equator, so their winter is in the northern summer, when Rio can be quite wet and cold.

Travel documents
British passport holders do not need a visa for Brazil. All you need is a valid passport, yellow fever certificate and some form

of hard currency (the US dollar is the best). Other nationals should check whether they require visas either with the Brazilian Embassy, or with their own embassies and high commissions. Some credit cards can be used, e.g. American Express, Diners, Visa, etc. The air ticket must be paid for 2 weeks in advance. The Brazilian Embassy is at Plot 257, Kofo Abayomi Street, Victoria Island, Box 1931, Lagos. Tel 612226 or 614386.

Please remember to take your passport when you pay for your ticket. You can get a Varig Air Pass for travel outside Rio if you intend to go to a number of places. For more information, visit the Brazilian Embassy in Victoria Island. You will not regret a visit to Rio!

Costs

This is obviously subject to change, but in 1989 the return journey cost about ₦12,000 for the executive class.

GREAT BRITAIN

London

London is included for the benefit of the non-British tourist, and has an enormous variety of attractions for the visitor apart from its excellent shopping. London has been at the centre of British history for centuries, and has many buildings of historic importance like the 'Mother of Parliaments', (the House of Lords and the House of Commons at Westminster), Buckingham Palace, and the Tower of London, as well as excellent museums, art galleries, theatres and nightclubs to suit all tastes. It is also an important communications and financial centre.

Getting around London is relatively easy, with the underground train network (commonly known as 'the Tube'). But, if you prefer to be above ground, the well-known red double-decker buses and the black London taxis are an excellent alternative.

Tourists can buy cheap travel passes at London Transport offices, which greatly reduce the cost of travel around the city. Tours to view the sights in open-air buses can be organised through your hotel. London is not cheap, either for hotels, shopping or travel, but the quality is high and some of the best hotels in the world can be found here.

There are many inexpensive London guidebooks on sale in the bookshops, with advice about places of interest and shopping, so waste no time in buying one, and then you can plan your time accordingly. The best street map is the *A to Z Street Map of London.* Knightsbridge, Oxford Street and Regent Street are the main shopping areas, and there you will find such well-known shops as Harrods, Selfridges and Marks and Spencer. The more exclusive shops are to be found in Bond Street and New Bond Street. Savile Row and Sackville Street are centres of excellence for men's tailoring.

'The City' is the commercial heart of London where the Bank of England, the Stock Exchange and Lloyds of London are situated. It is almost deserted at night when all the stockbrokers, bankers and office workers have gone home. The West End is where most of the big hotels, shops and theatres are, and it is the centre of London's nightlife. Kensington and Chelsea are two of London's most fashionable residential areas.

Tourist sites

In any city as large as London there are many sights to see, but the most popular tourist attractions are as follows:

a. *The Tower of London* and nearby *Tower Bridge.* The Tower has had a long and fascinating, if somewhat bloody, history. The Crown Jewels are on display here, guarded by the 'Beefeaters' in their Tudor uniforms. The tower is a 'must' for visitors to London.

b. *Buckingham Palace.* This is the Queen's London residence.

The Changing of the Guard takes place at 11.30 am every day. Also, you may be lucky enough to see the Queen entering or leaving the Palace. When the Queen is in residence, the Royal Standard will be flown above the Palace. The Queen's Art Gallery is at the back of the Palace and is open to the public every day except Monday. It can be entered from Buckingham Palace Road. The price for admission in 1989 was £1.20.

c. *Kensington Palace.* Kensington Palace is on Palace Avenue off Kensington Road near Kensington Gardens. The Palace's royal connections date from 1698. The State Apartments show Queen Victoria's childhood home, the birth place of Queen Mary (grandmother of the present Queen) and a splendid exhibition of Court Dress. The nearest underground station is High Street Kensington.

d. *Madame Tussaud's Waxworks.* This is a fantastic display of life-sized figures of the great, the renowned and the infamous, modelled in wax. They are so good that you have to look twice to make sure the figure you are staring at is not a real person - many visitors have asked for directions from the wax-work policeman! On the same site is the London Planetarium, with its immense panorama of the night sky, and a new Laserium giving a brilliant laser-light display. Madame Tussaud's is in Marylebone Road opposite Baker Street Underground Station. The Tussaud Group has recently opened 'Rock Circus' at Piccadilly Circus, which brings to life the story of rock and pop from the 1950's to the present day. The electronically controlled models 'perform' in a spectacular show on a revolving stage. The Rock Circus is open daily from 10.00 am until 10.00 pm.

e. *Cabinet War Rooms.* Sir Winston Churchill fought World War 2 from this underground 'bunker', and it was from here that many of the critical decisions of that war were made. The Cabinet War Rooms are at the back of the Foreign & Commonwealth Office, Clive Steps, King Charles Street, Westminster. They are close to Westminster Abbey, the Houses of Parliament and St James's Park. The nearest undergrounds are either Westminster or St James's Park. The admission fee is £3.00 and it is open daily from 10.00 am until 6.00 pm.

f. *Museums.* There are many excellent museums in London including the following:

    i. The *British Museum* - especially renowned for its archaeological and art treasures. It is in Russell St, Bloomsbury.

    ii. The *Imperial War Museum* - the history of warfare through the ages. It is south of the river at Lambeth Road, SE 11. The nearest underground station is Lambeth North.

    iii. The *Victoria* and *Albert Museum* - furniture, porcelain, glass and every kind of antique *objet d'art.* The Museum is in Old Brompton Road and the nearest tube is South Kensington.

    iv. The *National Army Museum* - the history of the British Army over 5 centuries of warfare. It is in Royal Hospital Road, Chelsea. Nearest tube is Sloane Square.

    v. The *Natural History Museum* - one of the best natural history museums in the world with life-like displays of roaring dinosaurs and birds, butterflies, insects and animals of all kind, including man! The museum is in Cromwell Road and the nearest tube is South Kensington.

    vi. The *Science Museum* - this museum has up-to-date displays of scientific inventions and would especially delight the scientifically inclined tourist. It is behind the Natural History Museum, in Exhibition Road, and the nearest underground station is also South Kensington.

vii. *The Maritime Museum,* Greenwich. The history of seafaring throughout the ages, in a beautiful setting with buildings designed by Sir Christopher Wren. Take a boat trip to Greenwich from Westminster, and enjoy a sightseeing trip down the River Thames en route.

g. *Art Galleries.* The major art galleries in London are the following:

i. *The National Gallery* - an impressive collection of famous paintings grouped into galleries according to periods, e.g. the Dutch School, the Impressionists. Situated in Trafalgar Square in the very heart of tourist London.

ii. *The National Portrait Gallery* - here you can see portraits of many famous people, including most members of the Royal Family. It is just behind the National Gallery, in Charing Cross Road.

iii. *The Tate Gallery* - another famous gallery renowned for its somewhat controversial exhibitions. This gallery is on the Embankment at Millbank, close to the Thames.

Other Tourist sites near London

It is difficult to select a few places from so many, but the following are some of the most popular tourist attractions for a daytrip from London.

a. *Windsor* is a historic and beautiful town dominated by Windsor Castle, one of the Queen's official residences, where visitors can view the State Apartments. Besides the castle there are many other attractions in Windsor. At the station there is a spectacular waxwork exhibition with sound effects, showing Queen Victoria's arrival at Windsor Station in the last century and in the theatre you can watch an animated 'performance' by waxwork models depicting scenes of the Victorian era.

Nearby, below the castle, is Eton College, England's most famous public school with its ancient chapel. There are some excellent restaurants and 'pubs' along the River Thames at Windsor, and boat trips can be arranged, up or down the river as you please. Windsor Great Park is an excellent place for a picnic and just a few kilometres away is Windsor Safari Park. Windsor is within an hour of London by train or bus. By car you reach it via the M4 motorway.

b. *Hampton Court Palace.* This was one of the Royal Palaces in the days of Henry VIII and is situated close to the river at Kingston-upon-Thames in Bushey Park. Its restoration, after a recent fire, is almost complete and fortunately nearly all the historic paintings and furniture for which it is renowned, were saved. The gardens around the Palace are a pleasant place to walk, and contain the well-known Hampton Court Maze.

c. *Oxford.* Oxford is less than 2 hours from London by car, but there is also a regular train service. It has one of the oldest and most famous universities in the world and is steeped in academic history. The Oxford Colleges which dominate the town are of great architectural beauty, built in mellow Costwold stone 'with gleaming spires' around immaculately kept grass courtyards. The chapels attached to each college are of great interest. It also is pleasant to walk, or take a punt, along the river, visit the peaceful Botanic Gardens, or browse in Blackwells bookshop in Broad Street.

Twelve kilometres north of Oxford is Blenheim Palace, one of the finest private houses in England, but it is open to the public. It was built for John Churchill - the 1st Duke of Marlborough in recognition of his great victory at the Battle of Blenheim in 1704. Blenheim Palace was the birthplace of another great Churchill - Sir Winston Churchill - the British Prime Minister during World War II. The furniture, pictures and tapestries in the state rooms are some of the finest in England. The Palace stands in 2,000 acres of land and has a library of over 10,000 books. The library itself is 53.8 m long. There is a Churchill Exhibition of Sir Winston's personal belongings, a garden centre, shops and a restaurant.

Travel documents

For EEC visitors to London, only a valid passport is necessary. For other nationals it may be necessary to have a visa. The visa may be obtained from the British Visa Office, Chellarams Building, Lagos Island, or from the Visa Office in Kaduna for those who live in the north of Nigeria. No other documents are needed and there are no currency restrictions in the United Kingdom.

Airlines

Both British Airways and Nigerian Airways fly direct to London. British Airways has a daily flight to Gatwick, North Terminal, and on two days a week British Airways fly direct from Kano to Gatwick. There is a fast train link to London, Victoria Station, (the Gatwick Express) every 15 minutes and the journey takes about half an hour. The British Airways office is in Commerce House, 1, Idowu Taylor Street, Victoria Island, Lagos. Tel: reservations, (01) 613004, 614003, 613664.

Nigeria Airways flies in to Terminal 3 of London, Heathrow. There are buses, underground trains and taxis into central London from Heathrow. The main Nigerian Airways office in Lagos is in Tafawa Balewa Square. The above may change so please check.

Hotels

London has a huge variety of hotels to fit any size of pocket. At the top of the range are hotels like the *Savoy,* the *Dorchester, London Hilton,* the *Grosvenor,* the *Ritz* and *Claridges,* and at the other end of the range is bed and breakfast accommodation. It is not within the scope of this book to give a comprehensive guide, but your travel agent will be able to advise you.

Tourist season

The best months are the summer months, from May to October, but even then expect some rainy days and take some warm clothing. The winter can be very cold and wet and is best avoided.

Tourist information

There are Tourist Information Centres at Victoria Station, Harrods Knightsbridge, Selfridges Oxford Street and Heathrow Central Station at Heathrow Airport. Telephone enquires are on London (071) 730-3488 Mondays to Fridays, 9.00 am - 5.30 pm. The British Travel Centre in Lower Regent Street provides information on all parts of Britain and has booking facilities. The Hotel Accommodation Service or 'Book A Bed Ahead' scheme operates from the Victoria Tourist Information Centre or Heathrow Central.

London events

The British Tourist Authority issues a brochure *The London Planner* which is a monthly guide giving the main attractions in London. Leisureline is a telephone information service giving a recorded announcement of events of the day. Dial (071) 246-8041.

VARIG
Brazilian Airlines

Introduces easy

USA CONNECTION

DAILY FLIGHTS FROM RIO TO MIAMI, LOS ANGELES, NEW YORK, CHICAGO AND EXCELLENT CONNECTIONS TO CANADA AND THE FAR EAST.

For more details, contact your IATA Travel Agent or

3rd Floor, Investment House
21/23, Broad Street, Lagos
Tel.: 660585, 660663, 660645

Leventis – growing for the future

From Kano to Calabar, Lagos to Maiduguri, the A.G. Leventis Group continues its long and happy contribution, strengthening the success of Africa's most important economy. Wide ranging activities spread across Nigeria's 21 states include . . .

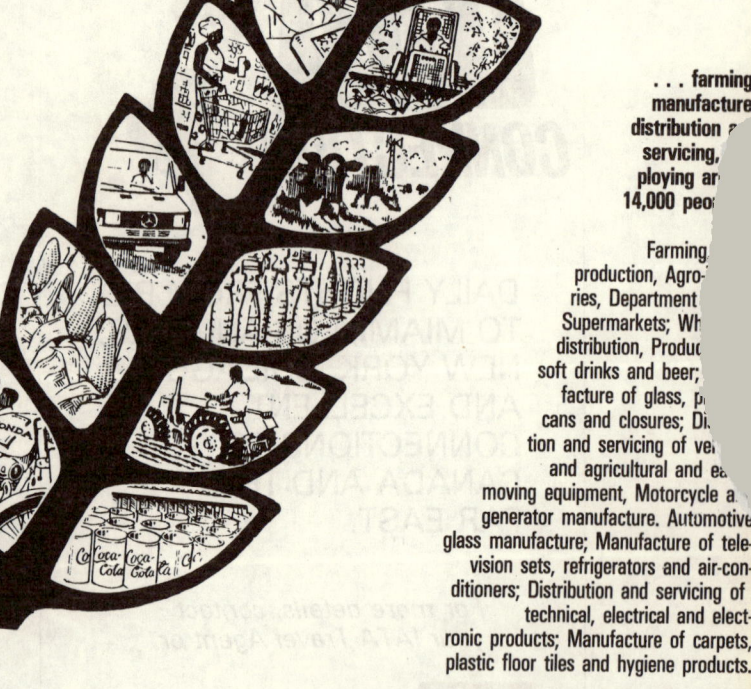

. . . farming, manufacture, distribution and servicing, employing around 14,000 people.

Farming, production, Agro-ries, Department Supermarkets; Wholesale distribution, Production of soft drinks and beer; manufacture of glass, plastic, cans and closures; Distribution and servicing of vehicles and agricultural and earth moving equipment, Motorcycle and generator manufacture. Automotive glass manufacture; Manufacture of television sets, refrigerators and air-conditioners; Distribution and servicing of technical, electrical and electronic products; Manufacture of carpets, plastic floor tiles and hygiene products.

A.G. Leventis Group

Head office: Iddo House, P.O. Box 159, Iddo, Lagos, Nigeria
London office: West Africa House, Hanger Lane, London, W5, 3QR
Tel. 01 997 6651 Telex: 24367.